The Pocket
Small Business
Owner's Guide to
Negotiating

The Pocket
Small Business
Owner's Guide to
Negotiating

Richard Weisgrau

ALLWORTH PRESS
NEW YORK

Allworth Press books may be purchased in bulk at special discounts for sales
promotion, corporate gifts, fund-raising, or educational purposes. Special edi-
tions can also be created to specifications. For details, contact the Special Sales
Department, Allworth Press, 307 West 36th Street, 11th Floor, New York, NY
10018 or info@skyhorsepublishing.com.

23 22 21 20 19   5 4 3 2

Published by Allworth Press, an imprint of Skyhorse Publishing, Inc.
307 West 36th Street, 11th Floor, New York, NY 10018.

Allworth Press® is a registered trademark of Skyhorse Publishing, Inc.®, a
Delaware corporation.

www.allworth.com

Cover design by Brian Peterson

Library of Congress Cataloging-in-Publication Data is available on file.
ISBN: 978-1-58115-918-9

Printed in Canada

CONTENTS

Introduction

I t is time that we all realized that all of us were born not only with the ability to but also with the inclination to negotiate.

Any parent of a young child of talking age has had the experience of negotiating with their child. The parent may not recognize it as a negotiation because the exchange is often so natural and seemingly insignificant. The perfect example is bedtime. By the end of a day, children often become more restless or noisy as they grow more tired. It is a signal to the parent that it is bedtime. The simple order "time to go to bed" is often met with resistance. Repeating the unwanted order seems to spark some reflex to negotiate. The child might reply with, "Please let me stay up longer. I'll be good." The parent might respond with "OK, ten more minutes, but you have to sit quietly." "OK, I will," replies the child. A compromise has been reached, a deal made, and a negotiation finished.

You can probably cite dozens of examples of simple negotiations that have gone on in your life, such as working out how you will spend a day with your spouse or friend, or agreeing with a co-worker on how to divvy up a workload. All those kind of experiences fit within a broad definition of the word "negotiate": to confer in order to reach an agreement. Conferring is nothing more or less than communication, something you do every day. All of us were born with the ability to communicate. Communication is not a process dependent upon originality or creativity. We are all born communicators. Some of us take the time and expend the effort to become better at it than others—that is, we hone our skills so we might have an edge when needed. The ability to negotiate is innate. The skill of negotiation is developed. Like everyone else, you can develop those skills, if you choose to.

One of the reasons that some people tend to think of negotiation skills as a gift given to only some of us is because as youths we were often inadvertently conditioned to avoid negotiating. How often did we hear our meager attempts to negotiate that extra ten minutes of wake time simply rejected with a firmer order to go to bed, or maybe even a threat if we did not follow the order? How many times was an attempt to work out a problem with a teacher simply rejected with an authoritarian rebuff? In our youth, most of us were faced with countless situations in which acceptance was the only option, because the alternative was either punishment or some other kind of negative result that we did not want to experience. Think about how many times in your life your attempts to negotiate were simply rebuffed, when all you really wanted was to confer with a person in authority about something that was important to you. What was the long term effect of those rejections? Most likely, they conditioned you to believe that negotiation isn't usually an option when an authority figure is on the other side of the table. Couple that preconditioning with a general tendency to think of anyone who you are hoping to persuade as having authority, and you have all the conditions necessary to lead you into thinking that you can't negotiate. After all, your earliest experiences proved this to be true, and perhaps your current experience often seems like a repeat of an earlier situation. It is a recipe for believing that you have no alternative but to take what is offered. The recipe, if followed, is sure to serve up unpalatable meals that provide little satisfaction and insufficient nourishment. In other words, not knowing how to, or failing to negotiate almost guarantees that your interests will suffer.

Decades ago, when I first joined the ranks of small business owners, I knew nothing about negotiating. I was a victim of my own ignorance. I felt that I could not negotiate with clients or suppliers because it would be futile. I was paid what the client wanted to pay me. I didn't strive for greater fees because I was afraid to lose the job being offered to me. Over a period of a few years, I saw that my business was not going anywhere. My earnings were static. I was facing the unpalatable meal that I spoke of above. I had the good fortune to be one of those types who did something when corrective action was needed. I found a mentor or two—successful business owners—who quickly convinced me that I was doomed to fail if I didn't learn to get what I needed from my clients, instead of what they were offering me.

I decided to change things. I read a dozen books on negotiating, and I applied what I read to my business. Gradually, over a few years, I learned how to make negotiating a routine in my business life. That knowledge proved to be invaluable throughout the years I operated my business and later when I served as executive director of a national trade association, and it is equally valuable now.

I have a simple goal for this book. I want it to help empower the small business owner to be more confident, more successful, and more profitable.

Chapter One

THE NATURE OF NEGOTIATION

eveloping your skill as a negotiator, like all skills development, requires that you understand the process. Unlike bookkeeping — a mathematical process — the negotiating process is not arithmetic, so it can't be reduced to formulas. Software companies provide programs that are intended to guide a person through bookkeeping. You probably own one of those programs. Years ago one software company created a negotiating program. That program can't be bought now because it was (and still is) impossible to create an artificial intelligence that is sophisticated enough to formulate strategies, adjust them as things change, and understand that things are changing as you speak. Negotiations happen in real time and space, not cyber time and space. So far, the only computer that seems able to handle the negotiating process is the human brain.

Step one in preparing your most personal of computers, your brain, for the negotiating process is understanding the purpose for, and process of, negotiating.

DEFINING NEGOTIATION

In his book Power Negotiating (Addison-Wesley, 1980) John Ilich, a professional negotiator, said: "In its purest form it [a negotiation] is mind pitted against mind." It is hard to argue against Ilich's statement. While negotiating is a process of conferring with another to settle a matter, that process is very dependent upon the mental processes of the parties trying to reach an agreement.

The negotiating process is one of communication: two or more people seeking to resolve a matter with an outcome that is acceptable to all. An agreement is reached through an understanding of the positions of all the parties and by balancing points of view. "Understanding" is a key word, defined as "to grasp the meaning or reasonableness of." "Reasonableness" is crucial. It is the core of all conscious mental processes, and it is the core of negotiation. Whether the negotiation involves a labor dispute, the end of a conflict, making an insurance settlement, or closing a business deal, the process always involves working with another party with both parties trying to grasp the reasonableness of each others' positions, and, if necessary, modifying those positions to make them reasonable in each others' minds. With those thoughts in mind, we come up with a definition of negotiation that reads like this: negotiation is a process of reaching a mutual understanding achieved through a meeting of the minds based upon the acceptance of the reasonableness of each other's position. Keep that definition at the forefront of your thoughts while planning for a negotiation and during the actual negotiating process.

FAIR VALUE

No matter what type of business you operate, one thing is certain. People you associate with will disagree. That does not imply that all disagreements are adversarial or hostile. Differences of opinion do not usually cause hostility unless they are rooted in some ideology that prevents the parties from accommodating each other's point of view. Fortunately, business is most often a practical matter, and very few business impasses exist that cannot be resolved through negotiation when the parties want to resolve differences in a fair and reasonable manner.

It is important to understand the basis of most practical disputes. Unlike ideological arguments, which revolve around abstract values, practical disputes are based on concrete values. Disagreements in business are most frequently centered on concrete values, such as money, timing, benefits, duration, etc. That is why most business disagreements can be resolved. The ability to assign a value to disputed elements of a business matter means that a corresponding value can usually be found to offset the disputed value. Time can be exchanged for money. Money can be exchanged for materials. The start date of a contracted job can be altered by changing the duration of the work or the deadline date. Wages are often described in dollars per hour. Wages are decided by a process of negotiating the value of an hour or the amount of time a dollar will buy. Being able to assign a value to an item makes it much easier to negotiate over that item. If you think about it, almost anything of value can be assigned a dollar value. For example, if a buyer wants his kitchen remodeling started next week, but the contractor is already engaged for that week, a solution might be an added fee to meet that buyer's demand. Is that reasonable? It sure is because the contractor is going to have to either hire additional help or work overtime to finish a job on time while beginning a job on time.

Understanding the relationship of values in negotiations, we see that business negotiations are usually aimed at equitably trading value for value. Done successfully, the process ends in each party receiving what they agree is fair value for fair value. This is sometimes called "Win-Win" negotiating. I don't like to use the word "win" in relationship to negotiating. "Win-Win" implies that both parties come out as winners. In my view, there are no winners or losers in a fair trade. So I like to think a successful negotiation as fair-trading. In business, there is nothing more honorable than making a fair deal: not taking advantage or being taken advantage of. That is not an original thought on my part. All good negotiators come to learn that quickly.

WANTS AND NEEDS

In order to make a fair trade, the negotiating parties must achieve a balance between their positions. To do that, we have to understand the limits within which any negotiating position rests. Business interests are best described as a continuum, with wants at one end and needs at the other. Wants represent a higher value and needs represent a lower value.

A colleague of mine once described his "wants" as his "whoopee" price, meaning if he received it, he screamed "whoopee" under his breath. He described his "needs" as his "whew" price, meaning he went "whew" with relief if he could close a hard-to-get deal at that level. By that analogy, we can see that wants are a desire and needs are a necessity.

Another way to visualize the difference between wants and needs is by considering your personal relationship to an automobile. You might want a Mercedes-Benz, but you need a car that runs reliably. The distance between the ends of that continuum are far and the options are wide. There are literally hundreds of options that meet almost every purchaser's ability to pay. What kind of automobile you end up with will depend on your financial worth and, yes, your ability to negotiate a good deal for yourself.

Negotiating is a process of moving back and forth between wants and needs until each negotiator agrees that an acceptable balance between all the parties' wants and needs has been achieved. Compromise is the linchpin of negotiating. Compromise is not a sign of weakness in a negotiation. It is a sign of intelligent bargaining.

Of course, you must be able to identify both your wants and your needs before you begin to negotiate. A want is an expression of a desire. A need is a necessity, that is, something you cannot do without. You might want a $50,000 salary while you need a $40,000 salary to meet your financial commitments. By identifying your want you have set the highest aiming point or goal. By identifying your need you have set your bottom line, that is, the limit below which you cannot go.

TYPES OF NEGOTIATION

In business, we generally experience three types of negotiations: terms-and-conditions bargaining, price bargaining, and dispute resolution. I listed the three types of negotiation in the order they usually come up in a business scenario. The terms and conditions of any deal are likely to affect its price. Therefore, we ought to resolve those details before we try to resolve the price. If we reach an agreement on terms and conditions and price, we are unlikely to have to resolve a dispute resulting from the original agreement. (Dispute resolution, unlike the bargaining over terms, conditions, and prices, is often adversarial in nature. In the worst-case scenario, disputes must be resolved in courts, if they cannot be resolved by negotiation.)

The three types of negotiations are similar in most regards. Wants and needs cap each end of the value equation. Bargaining over terms, conditions, and prices is really part of the selling process. In the salesman's language, it is called "closing" the deal. It is the process of listening to your client's objections and providing good reasons for your position or alternatives to them. Because you are trying to sell something, it is usually a friendly exchange. "Friendly" does not mean it is not businesslike. In business, amiability produces better results than indifference or hostility.

Dispute resolution is rarely friendly. It is adversarial by its nature, and that means it can become hostile. While hostility serves no one's purposes in settling a dispute, when a party feels wronged it is often difficult for him to control or mask his hostile feeling. One reason for this is because a dispute is usually seen as a win-or-lose situation. No one wants to be the loser. Where there are winners and losers, there is a contest. A contest usually gets adrenaline flowing. The heart rate goes up, and the emotions peak with the increasing beat. It is instinctive behavior, dating back to our prehistoric ancestors. Losing for them was likely to mean that they were going to be a beast's dinner, or maimed at best. Human defensive reactions haven't changed over the millennia. The reasons we get defensive have multiplied, but in the end none of us want to be the symbolic "dinner" of another, so we dig in for the fight, and we usually get one. The important thing to remember is that by conducting complete and proper negotiations in the early stages of making business arrangements, we can usually avoid subsequent disputes.

CONDITIONS FOR NEGOTIATING

Negotiating is dependent upon two conditions, both of which must be met before the process can begin. First, there has to be some level of disagreement between the parties' positions. If there isn't, then there is nothing to negotiate. I have actually met some people who like the challenge of negotiating so much that they will work hard to find something to disagree about, just so they can negotiate. Personally, I think one should try to control neurotic behavior in business, so I'd suggest that you resist the temptation to bargain unless you have a better reason than just because you feel like it.

Once there is some level of disagreement, the second condition is that the parties on both sides of the disagreement must be willing to negotiate. Sometimes, one party may not be willing to negotiate, preferring simply to move on if the other party does not accept his or her position. In that case, a negotiation is impossible, because you can't have a "meeting if the minds" unless there are at least two minds engaged in the process. Sometimes, a person will appear to be unwilling to negotiate. That is not always a sign that a negotiation is impossible. It is often a feint aimed at getting you to accept their terms without discussion. It works, if you let it. There are ways to deal with such a feint, and we will explore them in the chapter on negotiating tactics. However, when you encounter a person who is truly unwilling to negotiate, you have little to gain in dealing with him. If the substance of his non-negotiable offer does not meet your needs, you simply walk away from the deal, not the person. There might be a next time, and it might be a negotiable offer next time. Don't alienate a person who refuses to negotiate. Business dealings are always in flux. What characterizes one situation with one individual does not necessarily characterize all other situations with the same individual. Always be open to an offer that will allow you to meet your needs.

BARGAINING ISSUES

The issues involved in a negotiation are usually divided into two types: principle and position. Principle bargaining involves abstract issues, such as your business policies. Positional bargaining involves concrete issues, such as money, materials, and time. While principle and position are connected, they are dealt with separately in a negotiation.

By "principle," I mean any policy that usually guides your business dealings. Compromising over your policies is acceptable, as long as you do not compromise your ethical or moral values or legal obligations. Your business policies might include things like requiring an advance payment or deposit, or requiring that clients pay certain expenses directly, so you do not have to finance their work to a greater extent than necessary. Compromising on such a principle amounts to breaking your own rule. Is that OK? Some rules were meant to be broken sometimes. Remember, you are not compromising a legal, ethical, or moral value. You are making an exception to a principle employed to guide the operation of your business. Whether you break a rule will usually depend upon how important the deal is to you and which rule you are asked to break.

While purchasing my last car I found myself at odds with one of the dealer's policies. The salesman wanted me to fill out a form answering about a dozen questions before we talked about a possible deal. I looked at the form and saw the questions were designed to help the dealer place me in a hierarchy of prospective buyers. It asked about the kind of work I did, whether I rented or owned a residence, how I used my recreational time, any hobbies I had, and more. Clearly, it was meant to help them get a sense of my purchasing power, business experience, and general financial status. A person who owns a house, plays golf, lists photography as a hobby, and works as an accountant is likely to be able to spend more than a person who works as a data input specialist, rents an apartment, walks for recreation, and has no hobbies. I refused to complete the form. The salesman said it was the dealership's policy that the form had to be completed before he could get into a serious discussion. He asked me to fill it out so as not to upset his boss. My reply was to ask to meet his boss. A few minutes later the boss came over and showed me the actual policy in the dealership's sales manual; it really was a policy. My response was that it was an asinine policy, because all they needed to know about me before we made a deal was my name and what I wanted to buy. *After* the deal was a different story, as there were legal and financial dealings that required certain disclosures. I told the manager that I was not going to complete the form and bid the pair goodbye. As I headed for the door, the manager caught up with me and said that he was going to make an exception, even if he got in trouble for it. I laughed (under my breath), walked back, and began a discussion about the car I wanted.

How may people do you think fill out that form for the dealership because they are told it is a policy? I asked that question after getting to know the players better. I was told that about 50 percent of the prospects question the need for the form. Of that group, about 10 percent refuse in spite of the policy. I was also told that an exception is always made for those who refuse. Yes, some policies were meant to be broken.

By "position," I am referring to value level. You have one idea of value in dollars and the client has a different view. Your positions are different. The difference in positions has to be worked out, and there are ways to do that. Unlike principle bargaining, in which you have to decide whether a job is worth breaking your rule(s), in positional bargaining you are usually deciding whether you can accept a price, or terms and conditions, while still meeting your needs.

Positional bargaining can be simple or it can be complex. A simple bargain can be illustrated by another recent experience I had. There is a flagstone walkway from the driveway to the front entrance of my house. The flagstones are separated and held in place by a cement border, which over time deteriorates and has to be repaired or replaced. Recently, I decided to have it replaced, because five years had passed since it had last been repaired and it was once again showing signs of wear. I contacted three people who do that kind of work and asked them to stop by to look at the walkway and then email me with an estimate for replacing the cement. Within a week, I had three estimates. Two were very close in price, near $700. One was about 20 percent higher at $850. The tradesman with the $850 price emailed me photos of his finished work and a list of satisfied customers. I called the man on the phone knowing that $850 was his "whoopie" price; I wanted to push him to his "whew" price. After telling him that I appreciated his efforts to inform me of his qualifications, the fact was that he was still a good bit higher than his competition. I asked him to meet their price of $700. He refused, citing the fact that he did above-average work and earned above-average compensation. He pointed out that "above average" meant that I would not have to replace his work for many years. I asked him what was the lowest price he would accept in order to keep the job from going to a competitor. He said $780 was his bottom line. Given that the stone stairs (two steps) from my driveway to the flagstone walkway needed pointing, I asked if he could include that work for his price. He agreed. We had a deal, and I had a provider that offered plenty of evidence that he did quality work. That was simple positional bargaining.

Positional bargaining becomes more complex when it involves multiple issues, like money and terms and conditions. Here's another recent personal experience I had that was complex in nature. As a writer and photographer who has previously published four books and coauthored a couple more, in addition to writing hundreds of print journal and website articles, I was asked by a major website that publishes information for professional and amateur photographers to write a series of articles for their site. I indicated that I was interested and asked them for the details of their offer. In reply, they proposed that I write the articles for them and provide them with copyright ownership of the text. In exchange, they would include with the articles my biography and a link to my books for sale online—end of offer.

For me, there were two issues. The first was a policy issue, because I do not sell my copyright; I never have and never will. (This is not a recommendation. It is a personal choice. Instead, I license limited rights to use my writings and photographs.) Second was a position issue, because I do not work for publicity only. I expect to be remunerated the old-fashioned way—with money. After explaining my policy and position, we discussed the matter, and I explained why I had the policy, and why I made no exceptions to it. I explained that a link to my books was meaningless to me, because my books had sold just fine for six years without their link. I made a counteroffer that offered exclusive rights to my writing for ninety days and then nonexclusive rights to use on their website as long as they wanted to display the article. They accepted that. We then worked out a fee per article based upon word length. We made a deal by negotiating the principle issue first and then negotiating the position issues, which were generally based upon how word length affected the price per article.

So you see that both principles and positions can be issues in a negotiation. Positions are usually negotiable. Principles are sometimes, but not always, non-negotiable.

STAGES OF A NEGOTIATION

There are four stages in the negotiating process: investigation, evaluation, alternative development, and reaching agreement. For the most part, these stages occur in order, with two of them, investigation and evaluation, usually happening concurrently. Through investigation, you will already have gained some information about the client, the assignment, etc. As you speak with your negotiating counterpart, you will be receiving new information that complements the information you already have. You will have to incorporate that new information into your prior evaluation, if it is likely to cause a shift in your position. New information often requires that you re-evaluate.

All too often, business persons impede their chance of a successful negotiation by not knowing that the four negotiating stages require thoughtful planning with thorough attention to details and follow-through. Understanding the importance of each stage is critical to being a good negotiator, so we will consider each separately.

The investigative stage of a negotiation is nothing more than information gathering. The investigation is done by trying to obtain the answers to a series of questions related to the object of the negotiation. The circumstantial questions—who, where, what, why, when, and how—define the framework of the investigative stage. (In Chapter 3, Planning for a Negotiation, you will find a series of checklists and notes that will help you in gathering the facts that you will need to negotiate in different situations.) Obviously it is not always possible to know every answer with certainty. Some answers are going to be your best guess. But certainty is luxury in a negotiation, so you must become used to the fact that you never have all the facts. Business is a calculated risk. Fact-finding is a way to reduce risk to a prudent level, not eliminate it. Fact-finding leads to evaluating (stage two of the process) the information that you have gathered to determine what useful facts you have acquired.

The investigative stage, the first stage we should undertake in a negotiation, is the most often neglected. It takes some careful and considerate work. But, properly done, it will increase your power in a negotiation. Information leads to knowledge, and knowledge leads to power. Negotiating power is something that you should never neglect. (That will become clearer in Chapter 3.)

Evaluating all the information you have acquired for useful facts is the second stage of the negotiating process. You must determine how the facts might influence your negotiation. Facts are evidence of something. The question is, What is the evidence telling you? Logically, if you don't intend to evaluate the facts you have acquired, you ought not waste time gathering those facts. It will save you some work, but it will also probably ensure that you will not develop a negotiating strategy. Strategy is the product of your evaluation and its influence on the tactics you will decide to use while negotiating. As you assess information and determine useful facts, you can anticipate probable disagreements that will require negotiation. That allows you to formulate approaches to resolving those problems if and when they occur.

The third stage involves developing alternatives to what your evaluation tells you might be stumbling blocks. If you anticipate that a specific problem might arise during the course of negotiating, then you should take some time to consider how you might deal with the problem—that is, what alternatives you can suggest that might solve the problem within the parameters of the wants and needs of the parties.

The fourth and final stage of a negotiation is the agreement process. This is the period of time during which you will enter a discussion with the other involved party. You are expected to communicate clearly to explain your position, understand your opponent's position, and work toward balancing those positions.

PROCESS INTEGRITY

Negotiation is a process of reaching an understanding through a meeting of the minds. The process is one of fair-trading to find the points between each party's wants and needs that allow each side to accept a deal without feeling taken advantage of. The process is the same, whether you are closing a business deal or settling a business dispute. Initiation of a negotiation rests on the willingness of all parties to negotiate with an understanding of each other's principles and position, which should be dealt with in order of priority. Diligence in working through investigation and evaluation of the facts will enhance the probability of successfully reaching an agreement. Negotiating is a process, and, like all processes, it must be done in a systematic and thorough manner.

Chapter Two

TRAITS OF A GOOD NEGOTIATOR

The financial health of your business is stated in a balance sheet that compares the financial assets of your business to its liabilities. As negotiators, we have assets and liabilities of a different sort. We might better call them strengths and weaknesses. Just as we have to be aware of our assets and liabilities to stay in business, we have to be in touch with our strengths and weaknesses as negotiators, if we are to be successful at the negotiating process. We also have to be aware of the strengths and weaknesses of our counterparts to the extent that is possible.

Your negotiator's balance sheet is a measure of how you stack up in terms of the attributes that it takes to be a successful negotiator. As you read about these attributes, remember that attributes, like assets, are acquired over time. You may not have them now, but you can have them tomorrow if you dedicate yourself to acquiring them. The first step to ensuring that you possess or will possess them is to know them. Let's look at each of them individually.

SELF-CONFIDENT

You wouldn't hire a lawyer who didn't believe he could properly represent you. You wouldn't hire a doctor who didn't believe she could give you proper medical care. Your clients wouldn't hire a person who didn't believe she could successfully complete the work to be done. We want all the people who represent or serve us to be self-confident. Self-confidence is more than just a feeling of competence. It is knowledge of one's ability and a commitment to succeed. It is demonstrated in the way you walk, stand, sit, and talk. It is revealed in the way you look a person in the eyes when addressing him. It is a belief in yourself.

It is important that you believe in yourself as a negotiator, if you are to be successful at the process. You have to build that belief by a commitment to studying negotiation, learning its techniques, practicing what you learn, and understanding that self-confidence flows from training. Take a moment to think about the nature of training. The military is a perfect example of what training can mean to the individual. The soldier trains endlessly. He learns to instantly and instinctively respond to any stimuli. With several years of training under his belt, his confidence in himself has been earned by hard work. You have trained to be a provider of products or services. If you have trained well, you have confidence in your ability. The same principle applies to negotiating: You must train to be competent. As your training advances, your confidence in yourself will increase. In time, you will know that you can handle anything that can be dropped in your lap or thrown at you, because you will be a self-trained negotiator.

You can bolster your self-confidence by remembering your successes. Each time you conclude a successful negotiation be sure to make note of it with a few of the details about what made it successful. As you accumulate your log of successes you will gain more confidence in yourself. Having a reminder of your success is a good thing.

COMMUNICATOR

Negotiation is communication aimed at settling a matter. If you can't communicate, you can't negotiate. But don't think of communication as being the achievement only of a great orator or writer. The level of communication skill needed for negotiating is only enough to make your position understood by another person. A sophisticated vocabulary is an asset to an essayist or an academic, but it isn't going to make a difference in a business negotiation. Most business dealings are best done in simple, easy-to-understand language. Which of the following two sentences is easier to understand? "I can't allow myself to experience an excess of expenses over revenues as a result of accepting your offer." Or, "I can't accept this job on your terms because I will lose money." The point is this: It is better to convey a direct message in simple terms when negotiating.

Organize your thoughts before speaking. Good negotiators do not wing it. Remember, negotiating is a game of wits. That makes thinking very important. Most people are uncomfortable when there is a pause in the conversation with another. There is a strong temptation to fill a silent void by speaking. The danger is that by speaking before you really know what you want to say and why you want to say it, you will be inarticulate and therefore communicate your message poorly. Often in a negotiation you have but one opportunity to get your point across. Never lose that opportunity because you felt pressure to end a silence before you knew what you wanted to say.

Discuss the matter at hand, not unrelated matters. The issue in contention is paramount, so allowing the discussion to be sidetracked by spending time on another topic is not only time wasting but also can be counterproductive because it can make it appear that the issue is not as important to you as you claim. By staying focused you send a subliminal message that you do care about resolving the issue.

Propose a solution to any problem you present. Remember it is up to you to solve your problems. Your counterpart does not see his position as problematic and therefore is not reaching for a solution. You understand the problem from your prospective and therein lies the path to a solution.

Speak to the facts without being critical. No one want to be criticized for a position they take in a negotiation. If you criticize your counterpart, it send a message of disrespect, and that is counterproductive for obvious reasons.

Always speak calmly. An excited or loud voice can be unsettling to the listener. That can provoke a defensive reaction that brings on an adrenalin rush, and that can lead to your counterpart losing his calm too. Two frenzied people are twice as bad as one, and one can cause a negotiation to break down.

Be succinct. An economy of words keeps a message clearer. When a person rattles on and on about something, the impact of what they are saying can be lost on the listener. It is even quite possible that they will stop listening, and that is a disadvantage.

Listen attentively. Understanding requires listening. Enough said.

I know that most business persons do not spend their lifetime improving their verbal skills, as they are more intent on improving their business skills. Well, the good news that it doesn't matter. If you can speak the language at its most basic level, and you strive to be a better communicator, you have the verbal skills needed to negotiate. I am not saying that you should not try to improve your verbal skills if it is lacking. If an asset is weak, you want to strengthen it. I am saying that you need only basic communication skills to be a good negotiator.

Fact Finder

Knowledge is a key element of success. Information is the core of all knowledge. Acquiring the information you need to have a successful negotiation is a critical component of your overall effort. Negotiators usually refer to fact-finding as "doing homework." As a learning process it prepares you to pass the test that you will face.

Fact-finding has two steps. First you investigate to get every piece of information that you can that is relevant to your negotiation. Then you decide which facts actually shed some light that will help you plan a negotiating strategy. The process amounts to finding all the facts that you can, then finding the useful facts among the total collection.

I can't emphasize the importance of fact-finding enough. Knowledge is power, and power plays a role in a negotiation. One way to cultivate power is to be knowledgeable about the other party, the offer being negotiated, and your competition. Fact-finding is the way to acquire that knowledge.

Organized Thinker

An organized thinker is a person who forms his thoughts in a uniform and structured manner. He has a consistent and logical approach to determining what he thinks. As a business person you have a consistent, repetitive, and logical way that you approach the problems. That same kind of thinking must be applied when negotiating.

As a negotiator, you must learn to follow certain thought processes. The investigative and evaluation stages of negotiation are patterned—that is, they have an organized motif. If you want to succeed as a negotiator, you have to learn that the process of negotiating will be consistent from one negotiation to the next. The only changes will be in the issues and the people presenting those issues. You will know that most business issues involve the same factors—what you get for what you give.

VISUALIZER

Brain studies have shown that thoughts about actions produce the same mental activity as the actions themselves. Mental imagery affects the brain's cognitive processes like motor control, attention, perception, planning, and memory. Visualization is truing the brain for actual performance. That can enhance motivation and self-confidence, improve performance, and prime you for success.

A very revealing study of the benefits of visualization was conducted by a group of researchers in the 1980s. They were out to determine the difference in benefit between actual practice and visualization of the practice. They decided that the study would only have significance by comparing a sample of participants engaged in a single pursuit for limited period of time. Two basketball teams of equal ranking in skill were selected to be the test groups. The measure of success would be how many baskets could be successfully made from the free-throw line in a set period of time by each team. The variable would be the means of preparing for the contest. One team was to practice free throws on the court for half an hour before the actual shoot-out began. The other team was to visualize, off court, the act of shooting free throws, as if they were actually shooting the ball. At the end of the practice and visualization period, the teams engaged in the competition. Each team shot at an opposite end of the court, making as many free throws as possible in the same period of time. When the time was up, the team that had used visualization won the shoot-out by more than 10 percent. No one knows exactly why that happened, but it and similar experiments have proven that visualizing contributes to success and can be just as effective, if not more so, than actual practice.

Strong visualization skills are usually employed in envisioning a subject in a certain manner. Using this skill to visualize yourself as a negotiator puts an asset in your balance sheet. You have to see yourself in the role of a successful negotiator. You have to visualize the process that you will be going through to beef up for the game. There is little opportunity to practice for a specific negotiation, but there is always opportunity to visualize negotiating with another person and thereby perfect your skills and be better prepared for an actual negotiation.

FAIR-MINDED

A good negotiator expects and demands to be treated with fairness, and understands that treating a negotiating counterpart fairly is the only way he can expect the same kind of treatment. Books have been written about fairness in negotiation. The problem is that these books don't define the word "fair" or "fairness" beyond implying that an agreement of equal value to both sides is fair. Well, I can accept that as a guideline for deciding whether a negotiation was successful, but I am speaking of the asset of being fair-minded, not of fairness of an outcome.

Fair-minded means being marked by honesty and impartiality. It has nothing to do with an outcome. It is all about input, not outcome. Good negotiators are honest in their dealings and impartial in their treatment of counterparts. They apply the same principles and policies in all their dealings. It is a fairness of treatment, not of outcomes, that distinguishes the successful negotiator. By dealing honestly and impartially, and insisting on receiving the same kind of treatment that you give, you will do more to assure fair outcomes than by any other means.

How do honesty and impartiality merge to make fair-minded? It's simple. You just have to be honest with, and apply the same rules to, all. You don't take advantage of the weak, and you don't allow the strong to take advantage of you. You are honest with all, and you expect all to be honest with you in return. You are consistent in the treatment you give and the treatment you demand.

COMMON SENSE

"Nothing astonishes men so much as common sense and plain dealing." Those are the words of Ralph Waldo Emerson, a nineteenth-century American essayist. In this the twenty-first century, we frequently see evidence of dealings that lead us to believe that some people simply do not exercise common sense. Today's politics can serve as an example. As I write this book, the United States congressional leaders and the president are involved in a negotiation over increasing the country's debt limit, that is, the amount it can borrow to meet the government's financial needs. The negotiations have been going on for months. Now, just two weeks before the government defaults on existing debt, the negotiations are bogged down for two reasons. First, the parties have not been able to reach an agreement on what expenses should be cut or what taxes should be raised in order to reduce the deficit and debt over the years to come. That is a difference in positions that negotiations can resolve. However, the second pitfall is that some in Congress believe the debt limit should not be raised at all, and that, if the result is the government defaulting and failing to pay its bills, it will have little consequence. The best economists in the country have spoken out on the matter. Economists say that not increasing the debt limit will have disastrous consequences for the nation, and could lead to a major economic depression, which in turn would likely lead to economic disasters worldwide. Those opponents to raising the debt limit have not offered any evidence or authoritative opinion to support their view, however. For them it is a matter of principle; if the country wants to reduce its deficit, it must stop borrowing money and cut its expenses. There is logic to that, but is it common sense? No, it is not. It is not common sense to try to save the nation's economy in the long term by destroying that economy in the short term. The common-sense approach, when logic dictates one course and reality dictates another, is to do that which creates the least harm. There are other ways to reduce the nation's deficit over time without destroying the economy.

Common sense is exercising good judgment in practical matters. When common sense is overruled because a principle would otherwise have to be ignored, negotiating is impossible.

OPTION-ORIENTED

As mentioned earlier, negotiating success is often dependent upon finding acceptable alternatives to existing but unacceptable positions. Finding alternatives is nothing more than developing options. Most often there is an alternative way of doing something. The skilled negotiator thinks about acceptable alternatives as a part of preparing for a negotiation. Once you have developed your position, assume that your counterpart will reject it or some part of it. Then you develop alternatives. It is even possible that you will present all the alternatives initially, if all are equally acceptable to you.

Developing options requires that you either anticipate reactions to your position, or anticipate your counterpart's positions. Alternatives have to deliver benefit for both sides to be effective. If your initial position is rejected, it is likely because there was not enough benefit for your counterpart. If the alternative you propose is also perceived to be lacking benefit, it will be rejected too. Alternatives are not options unless they offer some benefit missing in your original position.

DECISION MAKER

The negotiation process involves making decisions. Each bargaining issue is evaluated, discussed, and decided. When all the issues are decided, an agreement has been reached. You cannot avoid making decisions in a negotiation. "Indecisive negotiator" is as much an oxymoron as the words "square circle." The competent negotiator is ready to make decisions and has a process for doing so.

Making decisions about issues in a negotiation is not rocket science. In fact, it is very simple, because by its nature negotiating is a process of balancing wants and needs. Therefore, as long as your needs are met, it is all right to accept the outcome. That does not mean that you should strive only to meet your needs. It is more satisfying to do better than the minimum acceptable to you. It does mean that decisions are based upon how close they take you to your bottom line. In the end, never settle for less than your needs. That is the basis for every decision you make in a negotiation.

Another trait of a good decision maker is being able to live with your decisions. Negotiator's remorse is not a good thing to have. Sometime you will make a bad decision in a negotiation and regret it. When that happens the best thing you can do is acknowledge it, consider what a better decision would have been, note it, and move on. Lingering regret undermines confidence.

COMMITMENT KEEPER

Once you have made a decision, you have to be able to live with it. Sometimes we make bad decisions that are irreversible. If you make a commitment in a negotiation, you have to uphold it, even if you know it was a bad decision on your part. You can always go back and ask to renegotiate a deal or issue, but you have to uphold your commitment if renegotiation is not possible or is unsuccessful. If you break a commitment made in a negotiation, you can be sure that you will not get the opportunity to negotiate with that particular party again. Sometimes it is painful to fulfill a commitment, but it is more painful and can be fatal to lose business because you failed to fulfill a commitment.

TRANQUILITY SEEKER

Tranquility is a state free of mental agitation or other distur-bances. It is easy to become disturbed with a person who does not agree with you, especially when you cannot under-stand why they don't agree. At the same time, mental agita-tion is the negotiator's worst enemy. An agitated mind is not a mind that thinks clearly. A negotiation is a battle of wits, or reasoning power. It follows that a mind thinking clearly is "wit-full," while the agitated mind is either witless or wish-ful. Reasoning power is the key to understanding. Mutual understanding is the key to successful negotiating. Tranquility is a key component of understanding.

EMPATHETIC

Unlike sympathy, i.e., feeling sorry for another, empathy is vicariously feeling what another feels and understanding the depth of those feelings. It usually requires that you have been in the same position as the other party, or that you have seen enough in life to understand the depth of the other's feelings. Notice that the word "understanding" appears as part of this attribute. Empathy can help us understand our counterpart's position. That, in turn, can help us craft alter-natives that might be acceptable to that party, or even to make concessions with the intention of cementing a relation-ship. A little bit of understanding in the first round of a nego-tiation can go a long way in making the next rounds easier.

Sympathy is something you might feel, but one rule of negotiating is not to adopt your counterpart's problems. You will never solve problems that warrant sympathy. You have your own problems. You can understand the other party and adjust your position accordingly, but do not cut the other side slack because you feel sorry for him, or you will be doing it for him forever. Business is business. Understand business problems, but don't cave in because you feel sorry for the person or company with the problems.

FLEXIBLE

There is a reason that trees bend in the wind. The alternative is to be ripped out by their roots. There is a good reason to be flexible when negotiating. It reduces the possibility that your negotiation will be uprooted. Flexibility in a negotiation is directly related to your ability to accept compromises by developing alternative courses of action. On the other hand, being rigid is the inability to do so. Reaching a mutual understanding requires that you be flexible. The world does not revolve around your wants or needs. It revolves around the understanding that outcomes are better when disagreements are settled by compromise. If you are inflexible, you cannot compromise. Unless you have some magic that the rest of the business persons in this world do not have, you cannot survive in business without making compromises. There is a great divide between compromising and selling out. Being rigid drives you off one cliff. Being too flexible drives you off another. Your flexibility always rests in the space between your wants and needs. Flexibility is altering your position between your wants and needs but not going below your bottom line.

INQUISITIVE

People learn by exploration, study, and asking questions. Much of today's knowledge has grown from probing by people with inquisitive minds, people who just wanted or needed to know more about what was in front of them, on their mind, or in their imagination. Asking questions is an important part of the investigative stage of a negotiation. There is no substitute for gathering information and for fact-finding in preparing for a negotiation. In a complex world of busy people, the best way you can find out what you want to know is to ask someone questions. (In Chapter 3, Planning for a Negotiation, you will be introduced to a series of questions that you might ask as part of your investigative effort in preparation for a negotiation.)

LISTENER

For the great majority of people, hearing is an involuntary act. You can't turn your hearing off and on—like you can your eyesight by closing your eyes. Since we hear all that is audible all day long, our brains have learned to ignore certain sounds, so we can remain undistracted, at rest, or actively listening to what we choose. Actively listening is an important part of negotiating.

The inquisitive negotiator asks questions and then actively listens to the answers. Most of what we want or need to know in a negotiation is available to us from our counterpart, but that information is useless if you do not listen and absorb it. All of us have had the experience in which we have heard a person say something but not grasped or retained it in our mind. We heard the words, but we did not listen. You should guard against this happening during any part of a negotiation.

Listening requires active involvement of the brain, not just the ears. It is quite easy to be distracted by one's own mental processes during the course of a discussion. Maybe you hear something that concerns you because you didn't expect it, so your mind drifts to that item instead of what you are hearing next. It is not uncommon, but you have to fight the tendency to focus on such a distraction. That does not mean that you ignore it. Instead, make a written note of it and keep listening to what you are hearing. Your note will remind you, at the proper time, to think about whatever distracted you.

PATIENCE

Patience is a trait that many photographers should work on. The high-speed demands of the profession and the desire to see images sooner rather than later contribute to a tendency of photographers to want to get things done fast. Impatience can prevent you from actively listening. It can also undermine your whole effort, because rushing a process usually impairs its quality. You have to learn to wait for the other side to come around. You have to wait for them to express themselves. Good communication cannot be rushed.

REFLECTIVE

Good negotiators are both thoughtful and deliberate, not only about their anticipated actions but also about past actions. Being reflective will help you in two important ways. First, in a continuing relationship, a thoughtful look back at past negotiations and other ramifications of the relationship can provide you with the insights into how to handle the current situation. Second, being reflective will help you develop a better understanding of yourself, including what you have done right and wrong in past or current negotiations. Looking back at your and others' actions, whether they took place months or minutes ago, is a good habit to develop. Scientists learn by studying past failures as well as their past successes. Reflecting on what went right or wrong helps you repeat the right and avoid the wrong.

ASSESSING AND ACQUIRING TRAITS

This chapter has focused on the characteristic traits of a good negotiator. You need to reflect on your own capability in this regard. If you find yourself lacking in some areas, it means that you have to stay conscious of the shortfall and work on improving the deficiency. Many of these traits are interconnected, such as Inquisitive, Listener, and Fact-Finder, or Decision Maker and Commitment Keeper. Allowing a deficiency in one trait can damage another.

The traits of a good negotiator are easily acquired or improved. It all starts with recognizing what they are, and this chapter has told you that. Then some self-assessment is in order. You will find yourself lacking in some areas and well stocked in others. You must focus on those you lack. These traits are the negotiator's assets, and, as your business cannot survive without monetary assets, your dealings will be unsuccessful without negotiating assets.

Chapter Three

PLANNING FOR A NEGOTIATION

Whenever you are striving to achieve a goal, there is no substitute for planning. Planning is an essential aspect of negotiating. Negotiators plan to have a defined course of action but also to avoid being caught off guard. Getting off track by a lack of planning puts you at a disadvantage. Surprises often knock people off track. Sometimes they even cause panic. Negotiating panic is a fear reaction, and it is usually caused by a sudden threat, an unanticipated attempt to impose a condition, or the uncovering of important facts that have not been previously considered. Panic is a loss of mental control, which means you do not have your wits about you—and you know how important it is have your wits about you when you negotiate. Planning is the way to avoid surprises. If you have done your investigation and fact-finding well, you are unlikely to be surprised.

Some negotiations require intense planning that may take days. Other negotiation planning may only take minutes, because you will have been down that path so often that your plan doesn't change. That will be true when you have repeated negotiations with the same party. Many of the techniques in this chapter will not have to be repeated when dealing with a familiar counterpart. Regardless of the necessary level of your planning, all planning starts with formulating questions that you ought to have the answers to, or at least consider, in order to negotiate successfully.

In your early school years, you were most likely taught the circumstantial questions: who, what, when, where, why, and how. Those questions might have been called the "investigative" questions, because all investigations aim to answer them. Now we can look at how to apply them in planning for a negotiation.

HOMEWORK

Planning for a negotiation is like doing homework for a test. It is a process of learning all that can be learned and deciding what is most likely to be needed for the test. The combined investigation, evaluation, and alternative-development stages of negotiation are the planning process intended to get you ready for the fourth stage — reaching an agreement. In school, poorly done homework can often make the difference between a passing and a failing grade. When it comes to negotiation, poor preparation can lead to an analogous result. Many business persons shy away from planning for a negotiation. They don't avoid it because they are incapable of doing it. Instead, they avoid it because they don't understand the process, or importance, of such planning. Like all planning, planning for a negotiation is best guided by consideration of the many things you have to think about before any negotiating begins.

SIX BASIC ELEMENTS

The most complex problems are solved by breaking them down into a series of smaller problems. These can be solved more easily than trying to answer the complex problem directly. The same kind of approach should be taken in negotiation planning. We can break down a negotiation into several elements and deal with each element separately.

Every negotiation has these basic elements: parameters, bargaining range, motivation, position, style, and priorities. By systematically asking questions to research each element, we can gather a great deal of information that will help us be successful in a negotiation. In each element, below, you will find remarks and questions that you should try to answer before you negotiate.

PARAMETERS

Every transaction is defined by certain parameters that must be considered before a deal can be made. That means the negotiator of a deal has to think about those essentials before beginning to negotiate. Some of the questions that can help you consider the conditions that might affect your dealing are listed below.

- How does your financial condition affect your needs in this negotiation? What does your balance sheet tell you about your finances? Can you refuse this job? Are you sufficiently bankrolled to hold out for a better deal?

- What would your competitors charge for the work to be done? Have you competed against other parties in the past for the same type of work? What was the outcome of that competition? What did you learn from competing?

- When will this work have to be done, and can you accommodate it? Are you so heavily scheduled that this job will overextend you? Can you shift a badly timed job to another day by offering an incentive?

- What resources (human, logistical, and financial) does this work require? Have you gotten a good understanding of what the job involves? Can you meet those requirements? If not, what can you do to supplement your resources to meet the requirements? Maybe you can team up with another person to combine resources. What is the buyer's budget for the work? How realistic is that budget? Has it been understated to induce you to keep your price down? Will their budget meet your needs?

- Where will the work be done? Is long distance travel required? What will that do to your schedule? Is it likely to cost you other jobs? What will be the effect of that cost?

- How much preparation, production, and post-production time will be needed? What fee is needed to cover those days that are not readily visible to the buyer? How will you explain that element of your pricing?

- What is the buyer's payment history? Have you or any other suppliers ever gone unpaid by the buyer? Do they pay promptly, or will you be financing them for months? Have you checked their credit and payment history with businesses and vendors? Is there anyone you can contact to learn about the buyer's payment habits?

BARGAINING ISSUES

The substance of any negotiation is bargaining issues. These issues are the specific items that have to be negotiated to make a deal. They are not the same for every deal, but some of them are part of all deals. Major bargaining issues in photography deals follow.

- What price is the prospect expecting based upon local rates and fees? Is that a fair price for the work? Can you do the work for that price and meet your needs? If not, what price do you have to get to meet your needs? What price do you think is fair? How will you convince the buyer that your price is fair?

- What terms and conditions should apply to the job? Do you have to post a performance bond? Will you seek indemnification from liability? Will you ask for a deposit?

- What are the terms of payment of fees and expenses? Can some expenses be paid directly by the client? Can you get an advance on fees and/or expenses?

Motivation

There is a reason for everything in business, or at least there is supposed to be. There is a reason why your client hires you, and a reason that you take some jobs and turn down others. It is important for you, as a negotiator, to understand the motivation behind your and your counterpart's demands. Understanding motivation allows you to construct alternatives to rejected offers and demands. These questions will help you arrive at motivation.

- Why have you been asked to compete for this work? Do you have a particular talent for a special type of work needed? Does the other party think you might be less expensive than your competition? Are you just one of many bidders?

- Why do you want to do this work? Is this the kind of job you want to do, or just one you will do for the money? How should your price be adjusted accordingly?

- Why should you accept non-fee value? Can you a testimonial or other promotional advantages, and what is that worth to you?

Will this job increase your prestige or exposure? What other intangible benefits might be there for you?

- What is the buyer looking for in his supplier? What are the most important attributes (like quality, on-time delivery, and staying within budget) the buyer is seeking? How can you intensify his perception of you in terms of those benefits?

- What deficiencies do you have? Is there anything that you might say or show that would shake the buyer's confidence in you? What might he focus on as your weakness in this deal? How can you minimize the appearance of any deficiencies, whether perceived or real?

- Why does the buyer want what he is demanding? What alternatives can you offer? How will those alternatives reduce the price?

- What kind of relationship exists between the buyer and you? What can you do to make the buyer want to work with you? What should you avoid doing to avoid alienating him?

- What could be the outcome of this negotiation? What is the best result that you hope to achieve from these negotiations? What would be the worst possible result for you?

INTERESTS

Negotiating parties usually have both competitive and complementary interests. It is important to recognize them for what they are. Doing so will provide an edge in the negotiation.

Competitive interests are easily understood. They are the bargaining points of the negotiation. They include things like price, deadlines, terms, and conditions. Negotiation is the process of resolving those interests.

Complementary interests are those things that do not have to be resolved because the parties agree about them at the outset. It can be very beneficial to review those interests with your counterpart for two reasons. First, it takes them off the table as issues. Second, it reinforces the positive side of the negotiation when it is recognized that there is agreement on a number of items from the start. A review of complementary interests is best done at the outset to set a positive tone. However, when a negotiation is at an impasse it can be a good tactic to refer to all those items not in dispute and point out that they make a resolution even more important simply because so much is agreed.

POSITION

Each party in a negotiation will have an opening position on the bargaining issues in question. The more that you can anticipate your counterpart's position, the better prepared you will be to deal with it.

- What do you want from this deal? What do you need from this deal?

- What does the buyer want from this deal? What does the buyer need from this deal?

- How far apart are each party's wants and needs?

- Where do your needs fit within the continuum of your counterpart's wants and needs? How can you tailor an acceptable offer to fit within your counterpart's wants and needs? What can you offer your counterpart to close the deal above your bottom line?

NEGOTIATING STYLES

Negotiators have different styles. These styles range between "hard" and "soft." One person might be either a hard or a soft negotiator all the time, while another might switch styles from deal to deal or even within a deal. Still others will be in the middle of the two styles all the time. Being in the middle is a good place to be. You have to be able to recognize both styles from your counterpart's behavior. You also have to be able to adopt either style when called for. As part of your planning, you have to consider the style of the negotiator you will be facing. You may know this from past experience, but if this is not the case, you ought to try to find a professional colleague who has dealt with the person before. In the event you can't predetermine the person's usual style, you ought to be prepared for both.

The hard negotiator is like the aggressive buyer. He is usually very direct, makes no attempt to befriend you, makes difficult demands of you, displays a resistance to compromise, often speaks loudly, can appear to be a bully, and seems as unapproachable as a mother tiger guarding her cubs. He is quite prepared to intimidate you into accepting his deal, and he will work very hard to convince you that his deal is the only way the deal can be made.

The soft negotiator is a good salesman. He is usually very friendly, tries to befriend you, makes no demands but instead offers suggestions, pushes compromise to make the deal, has a friendly tone of voice, appears to be tranquil, and tries to make you think he is working in your best interest. He is as approachable as a puppy dog.

Hard and soft are the extreme of negotiating style. Some people have suggested that the best way to deal with an extreme negotiator is to adopt the opposite style. If your counterpart is hard, they think it best for you to be soft. I guess that comes from magical thinking that business is like magnetism and opposites attract. Personally, I see no sense in that notion. While negotiating is an attempt to balance positions, it is not done by counter-balancing styles. It is done through compromise and even concession, until interests are satisfactorily merged to produce fair treatment for both sides. My advice is that when you detect that a person is giving you a hard line or a soft soap treatment, you should adopt their style. Treat them in the same way they treat you. If you become a mirror of the way they present themselves, you will effectively turn the table on them by forcing them to deal with a person who presents just like them. What usually happens is that they quickly see that they have met their match, and then they usually shift slowly to a more moderate and middle-of-the-spectrum style. If you act opposite to their style, the hard negotiator will see you as dinner, and the soft negotiator will see you as unreasonable.

NEGOTIATING PRIORITIES

The priority order you establish in your negotiating plan can vary from case to case. In most cases, you will want to settle the principle issues first. Sometimes you will work on the position bargaining as a priority. The particular circumstances of any negotiation will usually indicate the priorities you adopt. Generally, it is better to work on principle issues first, because if you can't get agreement on those issues, you are unlikely to get agreement on positional issues, and any agreement on positions is likely to be meaningless because the deal cannot be closed on principle.

Perhaps you are going to negotiate a very substantial job, which will involve significant expenses. You might find that the total of the expenses will exceed the fee for your services. Many business people will only finance expenses to a certain point, because they do not want to tie up their cash financing a client's work. As a result, they have a policy of requiring the client to either pay them directly to cover such expenses or pay an advance payment or deposit. In a situation where the expenses will be very high, and you are unwilling to fully finance them, you would plan to negotiate that issue early. Why? Because if you won't take the job unless some or all of the expenses are paid directly, there is no point in working to resolve different positions over other conditions or the price. The same situation might occur when one party is seeking an advance on expenses or a portion of a professional fee in advance. Here's an example: You feel that you must receive part of the fee in advance, either because you are concerned about the client's ability to pay your invoice promptly, or because it is a new client, and you don't want to find them to be a poor payer after you deliver the job. In this case, you would first negotiate the payment of part of your fee in advance, because without that all other issues are moot. Lawyers are in the habit of getting retainers, a payment held on account and from which payments are deducted as services are rendered. While the terms and amounts of retainers are negotiable, most lawyers do not agree to work with a client until a retainer is agreed upon.

In each of the examples above, you see a situation in which the principles are as important as the position. There would be no reason to expend energy and time negotiating the compensation for the deal if you have a potentially deal-breaking policy to put on the table. If your policy is rejected, and you do not feel that a compromise is in order, then the negotiation is over unless your counterpart changes his mind.

Your priorities in negotiating your positions are usually governed by two simple rules: 1) Resolve the easy issues first, and 2) resolve the fees last. The easy issues might be the duration of the job, when it will begin, and what the final deadline is. The more difficult issues are usually money related, like what the reasonable expenses for the work are and what constitutes a fair rate. You have heard the adage "Do not put the cart before the horse." The "cart" in negotiations is the compensation.

EVALUATING THE INFORMATION

As you assemble the information that will help you prepare some alternatives to offer the buyer, the process of evaluating begins. The answers to the many questions I've suggested in the preceding sections will begin to connect automatically. It is how the brain works. You feed data into the brain, which processes it in the background. It is much like making a spreadsheet containing formulas on a computer. You enter data, and the computer processes it. You don't see it processing, because it happens internally, not on the screen. The cybernetic functions of the human mind will begin to connect items that influence each other as you go through the list of questions and make answers. The evaluation of the data is underway as soon as you answer the first question.

It is important to evaluate to exercise common sense. Practical problems require practical solutions. If you need $1,000 to do a job, then no amount of magic thinking is going to end up with an evaluation that you can take $900.

The final step in evaluating is to get data on paper and to formulate some thoughts about your position. A good way to do that is to have an aid called a homework sheet.

HOMEWORK SHEET

A homework sheet is a form, and it is a good device to help in making evaluations for a negotiation. It stimulates your thinking and helps you to focus on important details of a negotiation. It is a tool that you will use when you need it. The more experienced you are at negotiation the less likely you are to need it in situations that become everyday matters for you. The major components of a homework sheet are discussed below.

Negotiation Homework Sheet

Client company: This is the company that will pay you.

End user: This is the company that will pay your prospect, if your prospect is an intermediary. This is particularly relevant if you are selling your services to other businesses that are acting on behalf of another party because the intermediary's ability to make a deal is contingent upon the deal it has with its client. Your prospect's budget is directly related to the compensation it will receive.

Client's contact: This is the person that contacted you. It might be a purchasing agent, owner, or other type of buyer.

Client's negotiator: This is the person who you will negotiate with. It might be an owner, salesperson, or manager.

Client's decision maker: This is the person with the power to sign off on an agreement. It is not always one of the previously listed parties.

Previously served client: Is this an existing or past account or a new one? If it is not a new one, then look up what you have on file about this client.

Local or distant client: If the client is local, you might be able to meet with him to negotiate. While this takes more time than phone or email, it is more personal and often more effective.

How client learned of you: This gives clues as to what a new client knows about your competitors in the area. If the client came to you on a recommendation, you already have an advantage. If the client found you in the phone book, you have no advantage.

Description of work needed: This defines the actual job to be done. It helps you decide the relative value of the work.

Special talent, equipment, or capability needed: This focuses your attention on what you have that another business might not have—in other words, what it is that gives you an advantage. If the job requires anything special and you have it, or if you can bring something special to the table, you may have an advantage over your competitors.

Deadline for delivery: You must know the drop-dead deadline in order to evaluate what time pressure the client is under to get the work done. You are not under pressure until you take the job. Time pressures on the client can give you an edge in the negotiation, because the client has to get the job underway and cannot waste time exploring alternatives.

Desired working date(s): These dates could conflict with others you have been contracted for, making it impossible for you to do the work. Perhaps you can offer an incentive to get dates switched to ones that you have available.

Prospect's special concerns: All prospects want good work at the right price. Many clients have a special need, such as a super-fast delivery, an assurance that the job won't go over budget for any reason, etc. If you can determine the special needs, which are sometimes fears, you can pitch to them and gain an advantage.

Prospect's stated budget: This is what the prospect says is its bottom line when it comes to fees. It is a guide to estimating. You can then give both an on-target estimate as well as an over-target estimate that allows for more or better work. Chances are that you will end up in between the two, which goes to show that budgets are not always what they seem to be.

Items wanted: These are the things that the prospect wants (but does not always need).

Items needed: These are the things the prospect really needs to meet its goals. These are usually, but not always, less than the wants asked for.

Prospect's payment habits: This is how promptly the prospect pays. If you don't know from experience, you can ask a colleague who has worked for the prospect, ask on an Internet listserv, or find out who supplies other services (janitorial, art or office supplies, etc.) and call those companies to make a discreet inquiry. Just call the prospects and ask the receptionist if he or she knows who the suppliers are.

Competitors: These are the names of the folks you are competing with. If you know the names, you know just who and what you are up against. If they are all notoriously inexpensive vendors, you will know that you are unlikely to get the work at your reasonable fee. If they are all more expensive than you, you know that either your price will seem low (and that is not always good) or you will have an opportunity to earn more than usual.

Competitors' advantages: These are the specific advantages that competitors might have, such as more experience, a more visible reputation, special equipment, capabilities, or facilities, or presently serving the prospect. The greater their advantage, the more you will have to sell yourself, and the more competitive you will have to be.

Your advantages: The other guy doesn't always have the advantage. Maybe you worked for this prospect, but with a different staff person—so you have a reference to give. Maybe the job needs specialized equipment that you have— so you won't have to rent it. Maybe you have special talent for the kind of work needed. Think about what differentiates you from the field, and consider whether anything might be an advantage.

Your offer: You know what the prospect wants. You have considered what the prospect needs. Will you give in to wants, or sell to needs? Maybe you ought to create three alternatives: one meeting wants, one meeting needs, and the other somewhere in the middle.

Your price offer: This is the price you will charge for the offer that you present. You might be offering different prices based upon different options.

Your bottom-line fee: This is the minimum amount that you can accept for whatever reason—and the best reasons are that you will lose money if you go below that amount, or you just aren't up to providing super bargains for stingy clients.

Advance on fees: Some jobs have very high fees at stake. If you don't know the prospect, or know it to be slow in paying, an advance on fees lowers your financial risk, but it may also give your competition an advantage if they don't ask for an advance.

Advance on expenses: You might want this for the same reason that you would want an advance on fees, or because the expenses might exceed the fees on the job, and it would be a burden for you to carry them for the billing cycle. Again, you have to weigh the financial risk against any possible competitive disadvantage.

Payment schedule: When a job will be of long duration, it is common to set up a schedule of partial payments as progress is made on the work. Of course, the first scheduled payment should be a deposit, to be paid before the work begins.

FALLING INTO PLACE

The evaluation and generation of an offer and some alternatives falls into place as you fill out the worksheet. On some large jobs this process may take many hours. On small jobs it may take only a few minutes. Regardless of which, you ought to be thinking this way on all jobs, large and small.

BEING THOROUGH

Like any process, planning for a negotiation requires thoroughness in the way that you approach it. Try to get answers to every question you can think of that might have a bearing on the negotiation. Become familiar with the many questions specified in this chapter. Make up a homework sheet. Then practice with a few hypothetical job offers, or go back and look at a past jobs and see how a more thorough investigation and evaluation might have helped. Most important, apply what you have learned here on your next job offer. Negotiating skills are honed by practice, and practice should begin immediately and be continuous.

Chapter Four

PSYCHOLOGICAL
ASPECTS OF
NEGOTIATING

The psychological aspect is an important part of negotiation because, as a mental exercise of wits, negotiation often involves things that affect our security. It also is a process that can require a person to exercise skills that they are unaccustomed to and therefore are uncomfortable using. The five psychological pressure points in negotiating are power, fear, risk, courage, and mind-set. Having an understanding and command of those five pressure points is a big benefit in successful negotiating. I have borrowed the term "pressure points" because it has a special meaning in both emergency medical treatment and in martial arts. In the medical world, a pressure point is a spot where an artery runs close to a bone—pressing the artery against the bone can stop the flow of blood. Medical pressure points are used to stop life-threatening bleeding. In martial arts, pressure points are nerve centers where the application of force sends shock waves through the parts of the body fed by that center. Pressure points are used to disable an opponent. Since the five psychological factors I have cited can either save or slay a negotiator with applied force, I think of them as pressure points.

POWER

By its simplest definition, power is the ability to act or produce an effect. As such, power is something we all want and have, but we don't all have it to the same degree. We know that some others have more power than we have and some have less. It first becomes evident to us as children, when most people tower over us: We know that they are more powerful. Oddly, we are usually unafraid of those more powerful people, because we don't recognize any potential danger in them. As we grow older and begin to recognize that not all power is used to good purposes, we take care to avoid people who might use their power to harm us. At first, we deal with potentially harmful power by avoidance. Over time, we learn that in addition to physical pain, we can also experience psychological pain. We are already conditioned to avoid physically threatening power, so it is quite easy for us to adapt to avoiding psychologically threatening power. The world of business is full of power signs, which, if imagined to be threatening, can lead us to avoid them. Fear of power in business is a real handicap to successful negotiating. Once we learn to overcome fear we ignore power imbalances. We learn to ignore power imbalances by understanding the nature of power and its limitations.

Power is a factor in negotiating. It can be a deciding factor, because the most powerful person can usually win, if he decides to use his greater power. That is one reason why negotiating is not about winning but about compromising to achieve fairness. Power, as experienced in negotiation, must be understood—so that you will be able to reduce the psychological pressure it creates. Fortunately, negotiating power can be analyzed and easily understood. Once understood the fear of power will dissipate.

Inherent Power

Inherent power is that which is bestowed by circumstances. The two most common types of inherent power are financial power and official power. Inherent financial power is acquired by birthright, inheritance, or good fortune. That is to say the person did not work for it. Just imagine that you won the lottery or were independently wealthy and did not have to work to support yourself. Without financial worries you could take any negotiating position you wanted to take, because your livelihood would not depend upon it. You would even have the power to be unreasonable without meaningful consequence to your financial well-being. Since you are reading this book, it is unlikely that you are wealthy enough to not have to work. You live in the real business world. It is a world where many of your clients have greater financial resources than you. In your mind, you realize that to some extent you are dependent upon their hiring you and transferring some of their greater financial resources to you. That makes them more powerful in your mind. The question becomes: What should you do in light of that realization? The answer is simple: Do nothing. It is a simple fact of life that some folks are richer than you are. So what. You would not be sitting and negotiating with them if they did not want something that you have. The need for, or desirability of, you and/or your services has placed you in a position of power. You have something they need and/or want.

Inherently financially powerful people and businesses do have dependencies. One of those dependencies is a source of supply. They have needs and wants that have to be satisfied by others. They generally know that it is not in their best interest to drive deals that make their suppliers unable to stay in business. The counterbalance to inherent power is the powerful's needs that you can fulfill.

Inherent official power comes with company or government titles like governor, senator, president, chief buyer, or purchasing agent. Here's an example of inherent official power. Long before Ronald Regan became President of the United States he was a film actor in Hollywood. If you liked him and wanted his autograph, and you saw him walking down the street, you would approach him and say something like: "Ron, can I have your autograph?" Move forward a few decades and he is President. You would approach him carefully because he has a host of Secret Service agents protecting him and he is the President. You would likely say: "Mr. President, may I have your autograph?" Same man, different office, but Ron is now Mr. President. That is official power.

Often, we see titles as much more important than they really are. Remember this: In business, a title is only power within the company that bestows the title. The president of a country or of a company can tell the vice president what to do, and she in turn can tell a subordinate what to do, but none of them can tell you what to do. If they want you to work for them, they have to get you to agree to do so. They have to negotiate. If you are the president of your company, you are at the top of the food chain in your company. If you are the sales manager, you are an important cog in the wheel. We all hold some sort of office in business, and we know that fact does not get us much. We all have to negotiate. Official power should be insignificant in your mind in a business negotiation. In fact, it should be insignificant in any negotiation, because you never have to accept the dictates of the other side.

Fortuitous Power

Some power occurs by chance. Fate often hands more power temporarily to one party than another. Imagine two opposing army units at war with each other suddenly and unexpectedly coming upon each other. Chance engagements happen in warfare. Suppose one army unit happens to be on the top of a hill when the chance meeting occurs, and the other happens to be at the bottom of the hill. Since holding the high ground is an advantage in ground combat, the unit on top of the hill has come by some fortuitous power in the engagement.

Business persons are often the beneficiaries of fortuitous power. It generally comes in one in one of two ways. The first is when timing is to your advantage, and the second is when you have an edge as a supplier. The best way I can explain each is with examples from my own experience.

At 6:00 PM one evening I was working in my East Coast photography studio when I received a call from the communications director of a West Coast shipbuilder. I had never done business with this company before, but I had sent them promotional materials in the past. Those promotional materials were photographs of ships in port in various situations. The communications director had a sense that I could do the job he needed. The company had a new ship that would be docking in the local port as its first port of call. The company wanted pictures of it as it came into port, docked, and was unloaded. When I found out that the communications director had called me because of my promotional materials, I realized that I had an edge on other photographers in the area, because it was very unlikely that any of them had done a niche promotion like mine and sent it to this particular company situated across the country. When the communications director told me that the subject ship was to arrive in port the next day, I realized that I had another edge. He didn't have time to start interviewing photographers. The job had to be awarded immediately. The deadline was working against the company and for me. I was the beneficiary of fortuitous power. I was, for all intents and purposes, the company's only good chance of getting what it wanted when it wanted it. I knew that my fee would not be as open to challenge as it would be if the buyer had a few days to find a photographer. In effect, I had no competition. That took some power away from the buyer and gave it to me. I used it to get a higher price than my needs dictated.

Another instance was the sale of a stock image that I had on file. A publisher sought some images from me to consider for use on a cover of a horse publication. Within the selection I sent was an image of a teenage girl sitting on a corral fence gently stroking the face of a red-bridled gray horse. When the art director called, he told me that that particular image was not good for the application that he had requested the images for, but that it was "perfect" for the cover of the premier issue of a magazine for teenagers about horses that the company was going to launch soon. I was told that I had the "perfect" cover image for the new application, for which the art director had obviously not yet solicited photos. This was empowering, because the buyer's perception that my image was "perfect" meant that it satisfied his wants, not just his needs, and by licensing my image immediately many hours of future work could be eliminated. I could close the deal before any competitors knew about the opportunity, and I could use the buyer's opinion of my image being "perfect" to great advantage. I did.

Your prospects have deadlines when they call you. You don't have a deadline until you accept a job. Time can frequently work to your advantage if it is putting pressure on the prospect have not only what they need but also what they want. It is easier to get a person to pay more for a want than a need, especially when the need can be filled from more than one source. Timing of events and selections available are two factors that can empower you on occasion.

Another example of fortuitous power is when you have something no one else has to offer. Let's say you are a seller of parts for heating, ventilation, and air conditioning equipment. You are the only company in your area that stocks parts for furnaces that have exceeded their normal life of fifteen years. In the cold of winter, no one wants to be without heat. When an old furnace needs a part in order to operate, the repair people come to you because there is no one else to go to. Obviously, you can name your price and get it if you stay within reason. You don't want to abuse your power, because you know that unreasonable prices will drive your customers away if they are looking to buy items that you do have competition for. All negotiating power has limitations.

Competitive Power

Competition is a fact of life in business. Every business has competition, and usually tough competition—that is, competitors who will do almost anything to get the work that is being offered. Buyers know and use this fact to gain advantage in a negotiation. They know that competition can be used to keep prices in check, and that by emphasizing the competitive nature of the business they cannot only prevent the price from moving up but also possibly even drive it down. It is quite common for a buyer tell you that there are a dozen other competitors of yours ready and willing to do the job. That is a veiled threat meant to instill fear in you. The buyer is simply trying to discourage any thought on your part of doing any more than meeting your absolute financial needs when pricing.

Let's analyze this kind of situation. This buyer who is warning you about your competition called on you for a reason. It is possible that the buyer called you because he thinks that you are the only or the best person for the job. In that case you have little, if any, competition, and competitive power isn't a real factor. It is possible that the buyer called you simply because he needs another estimate to satisfy the policy of his company to have a certain number of bids on any job. In that case, competitive power isn't a factor, because you are not going to get the job anyway. What is most likely is that the buyer thought you would be able to do the job competitively—that is, at the same price that other qualified suppliers would charge. In that case competitive power is a factor, but just how important a factor is it? In such a situation all bidders would have the same power being used against them. The way you overcome the power advantage your client has is to differentiate yourself from the competition. What do you have that gives you an edge? You will have thought about this during the homework process, and you might find things that make you perfect for the job, or you might uncover buyer concerns that you can specially address in presenting your offer. When you read about commitment, below, you will have one example of how to differentiate yourself when no obvious tangible differentiation exists.

Competitive power is either not a factor in negotiating, or it is a factor that affects your competition just as it does you. In that case it is an equalizer: It does not make your competition more powerful. The problem is that the buyer is the one who will be empowered, if you permit it. To deny that empowerment to the buyer, you need only to ignore the fact that there is competition, and make your decisions based upon your bottom line. You never go below your bottom line, even when your competitor is willing to work cheaper than you. Don't let your competitors set your price: They might price you into bankruptcy. Ultimately, if the buyer doesn't want to pay your bottom-line price, you lose the job. That's OK: There will be others that you won't lose.

Sometimes negotiators can turn the tables on buyers when it comes to using competitive power. It works this way. When you are contacted by buyers it is usually because they think you can deliver what they need. The contacts themselves should reinforce your confidence, because you know that you are desirable in the buyers' minds. You can influence buyers' thinking by letting them know that they might have competition for your services—that is, you have other clients, and you are not dependent upon them. There are two ways to do this. One is to use the technique described below under the heading The Power of Commitment, and the other is to let them know you are busy. When a buyer calls and asks whether you can come into see him or do a job on a certain day, you can always respond with some hesitation by saying that you have something else planned on the date, but that you might be able to change it. It might be done like this: "I do have other plans for that day, but give me an idea of what I can do for you, and I'll see if I can change them." You have not lied to the prospect because everyone has something planned for future days even if it is not written down. You have simply told the buyer that you have things that compete for your time and interest, and he can't be guaranteed that you are available to him. Once a buyer has selected you as a desirable source, he is unlikely to want to lose that access. The fact that he is competing for your time can make him more willing to make concessions when you are the person he wants for the job.

The Power of Commitment
People are usually impressed by those who back up what they say with some sort of commitment. That is why warranties and guarantees are often used to sell products and

services. Buyers are impressed by commitment. While I would never recommend that you guarantee anything other than that over which you have complete control I would suggest that you consider guaranteeing the quality of your services and products when need be. When might you need to do it? Here is a possible scenario.

Your competition's pricing is being thrown up to you in attempt to get you to lower your price. You suspect that it is a just a ploy and that the buyer really wants to use you. You want to call him on it and to give him a reason to accept your price. Here is the litany that I use in such a situation. "I know that some other suppliers charge less than I do. I also know that there is a reason for that. In some cases it is because they do not have the required level of experience, or the right equipment, or they just lowball everyone. Experience is important to getting your job done on time and within budget; using the wrong equipment will have quality consequences; and a low-priced supplier is unlikely to be able to afford do this job right. You won't have those problems with me. Here is a listing of my clients with names of contacts and their phone numbers. You can call any or all of them. I will pay for the phone calls. If you can find one person who says that I ever failed them in quality of performance on any level, I will meet the lowest fee you are quoted."

I have never known any buyer to call anyone on the list. I have never had to reduce my fee. I have closed many deals under competitive pressure by making a commitment that speaks to the hidden fears of buyers about missing deadlines, going over budget, or ending up with substandard work. Commitment works wonders in the face of competition.

The Power of Refusal

Refusal stops everything in its tracks. A final refusal in a negotiation stops all forward progress. No one can force you to make a bad deal for yourself. When the negotiation isn't going your way, when you see that the process is simply making a bad deal for you and you can't change that, then you are best off just saying, "no, thank you" to the other party and withdrawing from the negotiation.

All deals are not good deals for all. You should never accept a job that doesn't meet your needs by going below your bottom-line position. To do so is selling out to the other side. At that point you are theirs, and they have no reason to protect your interests. It is your interests that you aim to protect and promote in a negotiation. No one ever went out of business refusing a bad deal. Many have gone out of business by accepting bad deals. Say no, when you should and must.

RISK

Many people are adverse to risk, trying to avoid it at every turn. The result is that risk plays heavily on their minds, and they are unprepared to take chances to improve their interests. The problem with risk avoidance is that it can make one too cautious by habit. There is some element of risk in every negotiation. Business is often called a calculated risk, because the level of committed resources can be managed according to the level of uncertainty of results. Negotiating, as a part of the business process, involves the risk of not meeting your needs by failing to negotiate a deal. The thought of failing to meet needs is a psychological stimulus that often results in feelings of fear, which I discuss under Fear Factor, below.

The size of the risk you can assume is usually governed by two factors. One is the potential reward. Bigger rewards justify bigger risks and vice versa. The other is your ability to survive the consequences of a high risk. Risk has to be measured by the actual dollar amount at risk. For example, if you were given the opportunity to pick a number from one to ten and there was one winning number between one and ten, you would have one chance in ten of winning. Those are not great odds. Let's suppose that you would get a ten-to-one payoff if you picked the right number. If you had to bet $1 minimum, your risk would be one dollar for possible winnings of $10. You would probably take the risk, because you can afford to risk a dollar. But what would you do if you had to bet $10,000 for a $100,000 payoff with the same 10 to 1 odds? You would probably decline, unless $10,000 didn't mean much to you. The two examples have the same odds and the same ratio of winnings to risk, but the amount at risk in the second example is ten thousand times bigger than in the first example. The inclination to avoid risk grows because the odds of winning have not increased with the size of the bet. You calculate that ten-to-one odds are OK for a $1 bet but not for a $10,000 bet. Odds simply indicate the probability of winning. Risk should be evaluated based on your ability to sustain the loss in the event that you lose.

In some negotiations you might not be able to move a buyer to accept your position. You might consider taking the risk of refusing to modify your position with the hope that your counterpart will give in. As a good negotiator you know that you must enforce any ultimatum that you give, or you will not be taken seriously in the future, including the remaining part of the negotiation in which you are now involved. How do you decide whether to give the ultimatum or not? It goes without saying that when you declare a position to be non-negotiable (a take-it-or-leave-it demand), you are taking a risk that your counterpart will break off the negotiation. Before you do that, you have to be aware of the potential effect of the risk taken. You have to calculate the relative value of the job you are about to win or lose to determine whether you can afford taking the risk. If you are very busy with work, you can afford to take a risk, because more work will surely come your way, and you have enough business to survive the loss of the job at risk. If your business is marginal and you need every job you can get, you cannot afford to take the risk and ought not think of taking it. It would be a bad risk to take, because it could cost you dearly.

The level of risk we can take in most negotiations is dependent upon our financial strength and our ability to lose a sale without disastrous or seriously negative effects. So it is obvious that your success in a negotiation in which risk-taking is involved is dependent upon the strength of your business, and therefore it is dependent to some degree upon how well you have negotiated in the past and how much financial security you have achieved through those negotiations. It is another reason to learn to negotiate. The more successfully you negotiate the greater your risk-taking capacity usually becomes. Understanding the nature of risk and the effect any risk might realistically have on your business will help you avoid feelings of fear, the enemy of any negotiator.

FEAR FACTOR

Imagine yourself in your office doing your work. Maybe you are paying bills. The phone rings. A prospect has work for you, if the two of you can agree on the deal. You know you're going to have to quote and negotiate. At this point, the realization that the job is not yet yours sets in. You think that you could lose the job, and your disposition changes accordingly from tranquil administrator to nervous negotiator. Suddenly, the checks you have been writing seem more financially burdensome than before. You don't want to lose this job because that seems like losing money to you even though you might not make any money if you fail to negotiate a good deal. You start to worry about losing the money. The fear factor has kicked in, and you are at a disadvantage because your judgment is now based upon not losing, rather than upon getting your fair due.

Let's look at that situation in a slightly different light. Before the phone call you were not feeling insecure. During it you begin to worry about losing the job. What's wrong with that picture? One thing that is wrong is that you can't lose what you don't have. You have become worried about losing something you do not have. Losers think about losing. Winners think about winning. Good negotiators think about making fair deals, and when they are unable to make one they accept it as a normal course of business and move on to the next order of business.

Fear of losing, rejection, and financial insecurity are often irrational responses in a business situation. There are few, if any, situations in life—business or otherwise—that will have a catastrophic outcome if you are not successful in one brief moment of time. Still, many people seem to treat the award of work to be done as if it were a life-or-death matter. Let's face it, if your business is so shaky that not getting the next job is going to put you out of business, then you ought to shut down and re-evaluate what you are doing and how you are doing it. Until you do you will be living from job to job, and fear will overwhelm you. Once you are overwhelmed by fear, your failure is almost assured. You cannot conquer fear by catering to it. You counterbalance fear by being courageous enough to do the right thing the right way. Knowing you are doing the right thing is uplifting, and doing whatever is right the right way is even more uplifting. So when you become fearful before or during a negotiation, and it happens to everyone sometime, you should just stay focused on your duty to yourself and the fear will subside as the courage rushes in.

COURAGE

Courage is defined as the mental or moral strength to venture, persevere, or withstand danger, fear, or difficulty. Since we are talking about negotiation, a mental process, we should see courage as mental strength. Mental strength comes from three things: knowledge, practice, and success. If you know how to negotiate, and you practice, then you will gradually succeed at it. You will develop the mental strength to courageously face any negotiating situation and your counterpart therein. You will see that you cannot lose what you do not have. You will also see that negotiating is about fair-trading, not about winning and losing. You will understand the value of fairness, and from that you will have a moral center in your negotiations. With that accomplished, you will have both mental and moral strength and the fullness of courage that comes with them.

Courage can be bolstered by recognizing that if you are doing business successfully, you must be doing most things right. That means you are likely to have a continuing flow of business. If that is so you should feel secure in your convictions and methods. The more business you do, the more courageous you can become.

MIND-SET

Winston Churchill said: "Never give in, never give in, never, never, never—in nothing, great or small, large or petty— never give in except to convictions of honor and good sense." That is what I mean by mind-set: the mental strength to never give in to anything except when honorable convictions and good sense allow you to do it. The good negotiator perseveres in achieving a goal of a fair trade in which all involved parties feel that their needs have been met through a fair exchange.

Developing that kind of mind-set begins with having both the moral strength to not take advantage of another, even if you have the power to do it; and having the mental strength not to allow yourself to be taken advantage of regardless of the power you face or the fear you might feel. When you have the proper mind-set, you have harnessed the fifth psychological aspect of negotiating.

We have all been encouraged at some time or another to develop a mind-set, but we rarely hear anything about how to do it. I believe that failures of mind-set are caused by fear, the one thing that can lurk in our mind and erode our confidence in ourselves. When you think about it mind-set is really dependent upon self-confidence. If we truly believe that we are able to surmount any difficulty, then while we might experience fear we will not succumb to it.

Self-confidence is built through two experiences: success and survival. The more we succeed the more we feel we can succeed in the future. When we survive dire circumstances in business we learn we can weather bad storms. I once asked a prominent businessman how he reached his level of success. His answer was "One failure at a time." He went on to explain that everyone fails at some point. Some are so stricken by failure that they lose self-confidence. He saw failure in some dealings as an inevitable fact of business. Knowing that he would at times fail to achieve his goal, he decided that the best way to minimize failure was to maximize opportunity, recognizing that the law of averages would result in enough successes to lead to overall success. I asked him what he did to maximize the opportunities. He answered, "I spent more time selling. The greater the sales effort, the greater the opportunities." Now, that makes sense!

The best way to reinforce your self-confidence and your mind-set is to foster as many opportunities to do business as you can. Whether you are a company of one or one in a company of hundreds you will do better if you maximize opportunities. If you are running your own company recognize that the sales department is the most important department.

Years ago I did a series of negotiating seminars across the country. I had a scenario that I used to illustrate the effect of fear on self-confidence. It went like this:

You are in a negotiation for work you need because business has been slow and your reserve capital is being taxed. Your prospect is really pressuring you on the price. You start to feel like you could lose the deal. The fear kicks in. You think about those bills that have to be paid; you think that if you don't get the work, you won't be able to pay your bills. If you cannot pay your bills, you will not be able to get the supplies you need to do jobs. If you can't get jobs, you will not be able to pay your rent or mortgage. You could lose your business lease and maybe your house. You could end up homeless. You start to panic, and you quickly give in. You have defeated yourself through an irrational fear.

However, if you have a strong sales operation, you are never likely to feel this way because you will—by the law of averages—bring in enough business to survive.

NEGOTIATING DISCIPLINE

An understanding of power, risk, and fear—coupled with courage and the right mind-set—will assure that you have the most important intangible qualities to be a successful negotiator. Power should not deter you, acceptable risk should not dissuade you, and fear should not overcome you. Mental discipline is a product of understanding coupled with the courage that comes from this understanding; and the strong mind-set that it is better to walk away from a deal than to settle for less than what you need. Negotiating discipline is what keeps the good negotiator on track and making fair deals.

Reality Checking

A good negotiator is both a realist and a pragmatist. He does not indulge in envisioning fantasy outcomes, and he understands that a good deal is one that leaves all parties feeling like they got something and gave up something. That's right. What I am saying is that it is not a perfect world, so there is no perfect deal. If you ever make the perfect deal, you may have finally reached the point where the old adage proves true, that when something seems too good to be true, it almost always is.

While I posit that you should not be concerned about competition, that does not mean you should be oblivious to it. If you are going to be asking 50 percent more than another qualified bidder, you are not going to be able to negotiate past that difference. If the work you are quoting on is mundane and could be done by almost anyone, you really have room to negotiate.

Even though you might offer to reduce a fee to move a deadline to a more advantageous date, you will not be able to do so if your prospect's deadline cannot be changed.

My point is simple: Be realistic. Do not have fantasies about your position. Sometimes you have an upper hand, and sometimes you do not. Know the difference. Be pragmatic. You want to make a deal, and deal making requires common sense, not extreme positioning. Otto von Bismarck, the ruler of Germany in the 1860s, said, "Politics is the art of the possible." That is a perfect description of negotiating.

Never allow yourself to lose sight of the reality when planning for or engaging in a negotiation.

Chapter Five

NEGOTIATING STRATEGY AND TACTICS

Many people see the words "strategy" and "tactics" as interchangeable. This common misunderstanding results in a failure to evolve a strategy, because most people think tactically. Strategy is the art and science of employing economics, psychology, politics, and force to accomplish goals. A goal is usually composed of a number of objectives. Tactics are devices for accomplishing objectives. The good negotiator learns how to think strategically and act tactically.

A good example of strategy and supporting tactics can be found in the conduct of the World War II in fighting the Axis Powers in Europe. The grand strategy evolved around the premise that the best way to defeat the Axis was to severely diminish its ability to make war. It was decided that the best avenues to doing that were to destroy its manufacturing base so it could not produce war fighting materials and to cut off its oil supply since the Axis countries depended upon imported oil. No oil meant no fuel and you could not move a modern army without fuel. To accomplish that super tactics were developed. Super tactics are those that have overarching effects. The super tactics called for the bombing of Axis factories, fuel depots, refineries, and anything else that contributed to war-making capability. They also called for cutting off the Axis Powers' oils supply by capturing or holding territories with oil fields that were or could be used to supply the enemy. The Russians fought to keep Germany from capturing the oil fields in the Caucasus region of the Soviet Union. The United States and Great Britain invaded North Africa to cut the flow of oil from Arab nations. Those super tactical goals were than broken down into a series of objectives, which were the battles fought to implement the strategy. It worked. While Axis manufacturing capacity was often restored after bombings eventually the fuel to run those factories was cut off. In the end when the Germans were fighting alone in Europe they simply ran out of fuel. They could not run their machines, transport supplies and men, keep tanks moving, etc. A perfect example of how tactics flow from and support a strategy.

To implement their strategy in World War II the Allies had to employ economic assets, maneuver politically, and all sorts of assets from farming to manufacturing, from engineering to production, and from medical to war fighting. Lacking sufficient assets a strategy is unlikely to be implemented.

Your negotiating strategy is tied to your business strategy because assets are lost or gained through successful strategic implementation. You have a variety of assets as part of your business. Your economic assets are the state of your business and your financial health. You have learned how those things come into play in terms of taking risks. Your psychological assets are your understanding of and ability to use, and to resist the use of, the five pressure points we looked at in the last chapter. One definition of the word "politic" is "shrewdness in managing or dealing." Your political assets are derived from being a member of a business community. The more you learn about how that community of buyers and sellers does business, the more politic, i.e., capable of dealing, you are. Your force is the energy that you use to guide the negotiation. Someone is going to gain control of the direction and timing of the negotiating process: It might as well be you. You can force direction and timing by how and when you make things happen in a negotiation.

Later on in this book you will learn how to assess your negotiating assets and apply them to tactical situation.

DEVELOPING A STRATEGY

The first step in developing a negotiating strategy is to fully appreciate your personal and business assets and liabilities. The positions you might take in a negotiation are dependent upon your ability to take financial risks. If your business is successful with good work and cash flow you probably can take risks because you are not dependent upon any one job. If your business is struggling, you probably need more business and cannot afford to lose it by taking positions that could cost you a job on which your business is dependent. The unusual exception to the latter is if you are on the edge of going out of business. Here is my real-life example.

I was in the early days of my career as a photographer in the mid-1960s. I knew little about the right way to run a business, but fortunately I was blessed with a measure of common sense. My business situation was precarious; I had personal and business bills to pay that I did not have the money for. If I did not earn a certain sum over the next couple of weeks, I would not be able to maintain sources of supply. It could even mean getting evicted from my apartment. It was summer and off-season, so there was little work to be had. One day, I received a call expressing an interest in my services. After I had gathered all the information I needed to quote a price, I assessed my assets. I had so few that it was fair to say that I had none. I had two options: 1) work on a small margin so that I would have a better chance of getting the work, or 2) ask for a lot of money and take the risk of not getting the job. It quickly became clear that a marginal return would not produce enough return for me to change my situation. All it would do would be to prolong it. Taking a big risk and going for a premium price was the only way I might be able to continue in the business. I decided to go for a "whoopie" price. If I got it I would be much better off; if I lost it, my situation would go unchanged, and I would likely have to close up shop. I pressed for the highest price I could go for within reason, and I got it. If I hadn't, I doubt that I would be writing this book today. When you have nothing to lose, you can take a big risk.

Did I have a negotiating strategy? Yes, in a manner of speaking, albeit a simple and unconstructed one, which I formulated without realizing it. It was that desperation that allowed me to do anything, because risk was meaningless at that point. I don't recommend letting yourself get into such awful straits.

A good negotiating strategy begins with a good business strategy and then is built specifically case by case depending on the circumstances.

A GOOD BUSINESS STRATEGY

This book is not about business strategy, but it is impossible to develop a good negotiating strategy without a reasonably healthy business. Business strategies aim to make a business more successful. They are multifaceted and range from simple to complex. This book is aimed toward small business. A small business's strategy is usually not too complex. From a negotiating standpoint, the most important aspects of your business strategy are sales and finances. Finances are dependent upon sales. More sales means more money, which in turn means growing finances. The first strategic element in a negotiation is the condition of your sales effort and finances. When you have a successful sales effort, you can expect better finances. When you have reserve capital available, you can plan for higher risk. The first step to becoming a successful small business negotiator is to make a good sales effort and to reserve some capital within your cash flow so you can afford to take a risk.

The second step is to know what you should *not* do when it comes to work. Yes, I mean make a realistic appraisal of your ability to do a job. Spend time negotiating for work you are unlikely to get because you have no experience or no capacity to do that kind of work, and you risk driving a prospect away forever. If you get the job and fail to perform, you will never be called again by that prospect. If you have the good sense to decline and explain that you cannot perform the job because it is beyond the scope of your business, you will impress the prospect with your honesty. Then, if you emphasize the nature of what you do, the prospect is likely to consider you for that kind of work in the future. Honesty makes a good impression.

The third step in developing a strategy is to know as much as you can about the prospect and about the nature of his business. What kind of pressures is it faced with? Does it have a good reputation with its customers? Does it have a good reputation with its suppliers? What is the nature of the individual you will be dealing with? How did he act when he contacted you? Was he hard, soft, or somewhere in the middle?

When you are the buyer, there is a fourth step, and that is to evaluate the seller's approach. What do you know about his selling tactics?

Later in this book I give some advice about how to negotiate the purchase of an automobile, so I'll use the example of buying a car to illustrate a buyer's negotiating strategy.

When you want to buy a car, you should first acquire accurate information about the car you intend to purchase. You need to know the make, model, and options packages, and the range of prices that are being offered for the car with the features of your choice. Additionally, you want to know what dealer incentives and rebates might be available. You can use the Internet to do this research by visiting a website like Edmunds.com, where all of that information is available.

Once you have decided on the option package that you need, you should identify the next package up. You want to know this because the car salesperson is most likely going to try to sell you on a better package at a higher price for the car. If you can rattle off the differences to the salesperson, you will indirectly be showing him or her that you are an informed buyer—a car salesperson's worst nightmare.

The next step is to identify dealerships that sell the car you want. You should have at least three of them to force some dealer competition.

Next, you should identify a competing make of car with a similar model that generally sells for a little less than the car you really want. This will allow you to get a quote that will be lower than the best price you will get from the three dealers that sell the car you really want.

Unless you are going to pay cash for the car, you want to know how good a financing deal you can get on your own. You can get that information from banks. The dealer will have financing available, but it might not be the best deal you can get. Always seek a competitive offer to use in a negotiation. If you own real estate, you can also investigate the feasibility of taking out a home equity loan to pay for the car, which, being secured, is likely to have a lower interest rate than a car loan, and the interest is tax deductible.

Finally, you must research how they will try to sell you. You will learn that they will want to know what kind of monthly payment you want to make, and how many months you will need to pay the car off; this is because they make money off of the financing, too. They will also ask what kind of down payment you can make. Knowing this in advance will allow you to be prepared to be evasive by saying that you have no targets at this point, and that you will not have any until you have agreed on a price for the car.

Once you have all of that information, you are ready to start shopping. How do you go about that? I'll answer that question in Chapter 8: Negotiating Purchases.

Take the Initiative

The only way to gain control of the direction and timing of a negotiation is to take the initiative, state your case first, and let your counterpart deal with it. Otherwise, you are dealing with their initiatives, and that can put you on the defensive. The last thing you want to be doing is shooting down their suggestions. It is better that they shoot at yours. That way they don't get offended by the fact that you don't like what they have to say. Your grasp of the negotiating process makes it easy for you to understand that your ideas will be shot at and some will be shot down—but you know this is part of the process, so you will not take offense.

Formulate what will be your opening pitch as you present your offer. Thinking about the previously mentioned stratagems in light of the negotiating principles you now understand. Remember that business negotiations are part of selling. You have to lay the groundwork so that your price offer will be appreciated in the context of the entire deal with all its terms and condition.

The tactical means to implement your strategy will become clear to you later in this chapter. It is important to understand that you need to practice your pitch so that you do not stumble as you present it. Part of taking control is to have a commanding presence—that is, to act authoritatively. Commitment and resolve are as much expressed by one's stature and voice as by one's words. Practice improves both. Remember, you have about thirty seconds to impress the party when you first meet. You initial message should not take longer than that.

Here is my opening when I meet a prospect I have not previously worked for:

> Good morning. I want to thank you for this opportunity to qualify for working for you on the assignment you have available. I assume you called me because you already know that I can do it successfully. If not, I'm ready to demonstrate that I can. If you have any questions for me, I am happy to answer them. If not, I have a few for you. I have to ask them to make sure I can do the work you want right. Any questions?

That statement takes just under thirty seconds when spoken at a normal pace. In it I tell the prospect that I am qualified and he probably knows that, thus reinforcing confidence. I provide him the opportunity to question or even challenge me. I set the stage for questioning him about the job. The I turn it back to him to see what he has to say. I take the initiative, but not in an aggressive manner.

TACTICAL NEGOTIATING

Tactics are devices for accomplishing objectives, and there are many such devices available to the negotiator. Every skilled negotiator uses tactics to improve his or her position in a negotiation. The need for some tactics occurs when a negotiation bogs down and the parties are stuck on an issue. Other tactics are part of every negotiation. The most useful and appropriate negotiating tactics are easy to grasp and employ.

Look and Act Confident

Look the prospect in the eye when you're talking. Stand or sit up straight. Don't lean up against the wall or hang your head down like you need support. Look confident. Speak with a strong but low voice. Slouching in a chair, leaning over a table, or burying your head in your hands can be seen as signs of weakness. Just as talking too loudly is a sign of aggressiveness, talking too softly is seen as a sign of weakness. Avoid any behavior that makes you look less than absolutely confident that your position is sound, correct, and to be adopted by all.

It is especially important to look your best and act confident the first time you meet someone. A person's basic opinion of you is formed in the first thirty seconds of a meeting. During that thirty seconds if you make a bad first impression, it can take years to correct it. That is why you need a thirty second pitch like the one I wrote above.

Look successful. Wear neat and unworn clothing. You don't have to look like a Wall Street banker. Just look like a successful businessperson. People are attracted to success. Looking successful contributes to making that impression. I am reminded of a story a communications director (CD) once told me. He was awarding a $10,000 annual report photography assignment. He interviewed four photographers. Two, including me, were considered capable of doing the job based upon portfolios. I got the job. I asked why me and not him? The answer was illuminating. The CD told me that my competitor has come to the interview in jeans that had a hole in the knee and a tee shirt. The CD said to me: "If I am going to pay a photographer $10,000 I'd like to think that he at some time in his life had $10,000. If that fellow had it, he should have bought at least some new jeans and polo shirt. I don't want him in the executive offices looking like that." I had worn a pressed pair of khaki trousers, pole shirt and blue blazer to the interview. It pays to reflect an image that your client will not be uncomfortable with.

Be Clear

Say what you have to say clearly, and don't send out confusing signals. I often hear a person say: " yes and no" or "yes but." Think about that for a second. They are saying either "yes with conditions" or "no." One thing I learned in an embarrassing moment was not to send confusing signals. I once said "yes and no" to a prospect. His immediate retort was: "Which is it: yes or no?" If you have conditions to saying yes, it is better to say something like "I can't say yes to that because of some concerns." Then explain your concerns. If you don't like a prospect's offer, and you have an alternative as a counteroffer, say, "No, I can't accept that, but I have an alternative." If something is unacceptable, simply say it is unacceptable. That is OK in business. Don't try to sugarcoat the fact that you won't accept something. Doing so can make the prospect think that you might give in if they hold fast. It's better to let them know where you really stand and how firmly.

Likewise, if you like something the prospect has said, let them know it. Have some catchphrases ready. Here are a few.

That's very enticing.

That is very persuasive.

More than fair.

Works for me.

They are short and to the point.

Ask Why

The word "why" can be a game changer because it asks for a reason and that means reasoning should prevail. As I wrote earlier, good negotiators are reasonable.

If you are presented with a demand that you cannot accept, rather than rejecting it immediately, it is better to ask why such a demand is being made. That forces the other party to think about the reason. Sometimes people have not considered the reasoning behind a position. Instead they acted impulsively or on a lark. Asking why can make them backtrack.

Once you ask "why," use your good listening skills to take in the reasons for it.

Understanding the reasoning behind a demand is the key to being able to create an alternative. If the answer you receive doesn't answer the question, simply point that out. This most often happens when a prospect answers your question with something to the effect of "Because my boss wants it," or "that's the way we do business." Indeed that may be true but true does not mean reasonable. The next question from you has to be why his boss wants it, or why they do business that way.

You have to be diplomatic when asking "Why?" It tends to put people on the spot, and that can get them edgy. I have a way of getting to "why" that keeps the negotiation running smoothly. Here is a sample dialogue.

Prospect: *"Because we do business that way."*

Me: *"May I ask you a question?*

Prospect: *"Go ahead."*

Me: *"Why do you do business that way?"*

Prospect: *"It keeps things simple."*

Me: *"This is a complex deal, and 'simple' does not mean 'fitting' or 'fair.' Let's explore a way around this."*

In this dialogue, I asked for permission to ask a question. Being granted that permission made it OK for me to put the person on the spot. Once he is on that spot, I can push for an alternative.

Unless you know the reason behind a demand that is leading to disagreement, you cannot resolve it. Once you know that reason, you have a chance at resolution. If you don't get the answer, diplomatically repeat the question again, stressing how important it is for you to understand why a party wants something, so that you can try to understand why you should agree to it or whether you might be able to propose an option that is acceptable to all. If the prospect does not offer a good explanation for an unreasonable demand or show a willingness to explore alternatives, you might want to consider dropping out of the process. Unreasonable people are not the best kind to do business with.

Be Silent

Silence is deafening at times. Many people become uncomfortable during long moments of silence. Often they will start talking just to break the silence. You never know where that talking will lead. After you ask any question be silent and wait for an answer. That puts pressure on the other person to answer, and if they are uncomfortable with silence they are likely to give up the information you want.

Listening is active. Hearing is passive. You cannot turn off your hearing. You cannot listen while you're talking. Your silence places all the pressure on your counterpart for the moment. You have asked a reasonable question, and he knows you are entitled to a reasonable answer. If his demand was more bluster than need, the prospect may be unable to give a good answer. This often results in his being more prepared to compromise, because you have shown him the weakness of his position with a simple tactical question followed by a silent demand for an answer.

Silence can also be asked for. In a tense negotiation it is not uncommon for one person to cut off another person who is talking. If that happens more than once or twice don't be afraid to ask them to be silent until you finish making your point. Call attention to the fact that you maintain silence when they are talking. You have a right to be heard without interruption. Sometimes you have to assert a right.

Broken Record

This tactic amounts to repeatedly asking for what you want until you get it. My best experiences using this tactic were when I asked for an advance on expenses, which I did anytime the expenses on a job would be over a certain amount. I'd start by making a unilateral assumption that I would be getting the advance: "Of course, I'll be billing you for half the expenses in advance of the job, because they are so high." If the reply was not simply "OK," I'd restate my demand: "The expenses on this job are really high. You are asking me to tie up a lot of cash on this job until I get paid. I really need an advance on the expenses." If I got another rebuff, like "We don't customarily give advances," I'd reply with "I appreciate that fact, but I need an advance on this job. I am asking you to make an exception. Fifty percent is reasonable, isn't it?" If the reply remains a "no," then ask for a lesser amount. If the "no" persists, ask what kind of advance they think is fair. Of course, you can push a good thing too far. If the broken record is starting to annoy the prospect, turn off the player—that is, drop the demand unless you absolutely cannot do the job without the advance, in which case just tell them that and explain that this is why you keep asking for it.

Bold Response

Prospects can try to back you into a corner in a power play. The most common is the threat to use a competitor unless you agree to the prospect's terms. Knowing that this is usually a bluff, a good way to deal with it is to simply call the bluff. Perhaps your client says, "Your competition will do this job for half your price." You can try a reply of this sort: "If you really don't think I'm the right person for this job, I'll be happy to step aside. I know I'm the best person for this job, but if you don't agree, I can't argue with you. If you want to use my competitor, it is your option, but if you want to use me, we have to come to terms."

To some that may seem like the kiss of death for the supplier, but it is not. When you have a prospect that acts like that you might very well be better off without him. Unreasonable pressure before a job is awarded usually means more unreasonable pressure after it is awarded. Additionally, if you let your competition set your price you have lost control of your business. Once that happens you are destined to fail. It is OK to make a bold statement when the prospect fails to be reasonable. It s better than trying to negotiate with an unreasonable person.

Trial Balloon

This tactic is used it to test the waters without putting your client on the spot. For example, "What would you say if I told you this job was going cost $3,000 and takes 3 weeks to finish the job?" You have presented a "what if" question. By doing so you minimize the risk and leave yourself a chance to recover from a rejection. You haven't presented it as a demand, but rather as a test. If the reaction is favorable, you can adopt the position. If the reaction is unfavorable, you turn the table by asking something like "What is the problem the price or the completion date?" If it is the price you offer to lower with an extension of the deadline. If it is the deadline, you offer to finish it sooner but it will cost a bit more. That takes quick thinking, but the more you negotiate the quicker you learn to think.

Another answer could be: "You obviously have a number and delivery date in mind. Tell me, what are they, and do you think it is a fair price based upon the delivery date?" You have just asked the prospect for a justification based upon his rejection of your trial balloon. Once you hear his answer, you have to alter your position accordingly. Note I did not say agree. I said alter. You tested your position without standing firm and it was rejected. You turned the tables and got the prospect to commit to something. That means you now have a negotiating range between your trial offer and his reply.

Use Candor

Candor is an excellent tactic that fits neatly into a time when you need to bring a negotiating discussion that has been going in circles to a conclusion. For example, let's say that you have been haggling over price with neither side giving ground. The discussion is going nowhere. You might say something like this: "I appreciate you want to hold to your position on price for this job, but I simply cannot accept it. I really believe that the quality of my work and the reliability of my service are worth more than that. I do want to do your work, I really do, but I cannot undersell myself to get it. It isn't fair to me or my other clients who paid my fees in the past or will pay them in the future. It is also not fair to you. If I work for your offer, I am likely to feel bad about my accepting, and might affect my work. I don't want to do that to you." You can follow that up with a compromise offer in a trial balloon. You immediately segue into something like this: "How do you feel about a compromise that will give me my price while getting the work done sooner and faster? I'll move the job up and put more time into it. You get it sooner and faster, and I get the price I need." You haven't demanded that switch. You haven't taken the debated propositions off the table. You have expressed your point of view candidly, and offered a compromise. That is, after all else is said and done, what negotiating is all about.

Nibbling

This tactic is employed after you've made the deal and have the job. Here is an example. My daughter was buying a hybrid car recently. She had never bought a car before and asked me to go with her. Once we had the dealer of choice selected based upon price which had been negotiated in the manner I describe later in the book, the salesman had to go confirm the deal with his manager. I suggested that when he came back with an approval, which was clearly going to happen, she should say something like: "Frank, you know what would make this a deal that I want to tell all my friends and work colleagues about?" "What's that?" Frank replied. "How about throwing in one of those roll up covers that hide what is in the hatchback? It costs $180 retail but we both know your cost is half that. Ninety dollars for a real solid word-of-mouth advertising has to be worth it." Frank thought for a moment, then went back to the manager. Two minutes later he returned smiling. My daughter hooked a fish on a nibble. If Frank had said no, it would have meant nothing because the deal was already done.

Optional Offer

I have already said that a good negotiator is option oriented. Options are the cogs and gears of negotiating. They make wheels turn. Here is an example of one I experienced. An existing client of mine wanted me to write and photograph his new website's content. I wanted to do it because he is a good client, pays on time, is reasonable, and reliable. No one wants to lose that kind of client. He told me about what he wanted the new website to be. He had a clear picture of the site's topics in his mind. It was realistic, and I wanted to do it. When I gave him a price he was a bit hesitant. I asked him why. In reply he told me that the quotes he was getting from web designers was so high that when added to my price the project exceeded the budgetary allotment for the project. Breaking the code, I knew that the web design quotes exceeded my price. He eventually confirmed that.

I offered an option. I would get a better price for him from a web designer I knew and had worked with. Both the web designer and I would guarantee satisfaction for a set fee with no escalations over the quoted price, and I would do all the coordinating with the web designer as part of my fee, which I did not increase. He agreed conditionally dependent upon the web design price I could get him.

A week later I called him with a web design fee that was lower that those he had received. I was able to get a lower fee because the designer knew I was the insulation between him and the client. He would have no client hassles to deal with.

I also got a 10 percent commission on his fee since I sold the job for him. That would pay for the time I would have to spend on the web design portion of the project. When told the price my client said he would have the $4,000 deposit check ready in the morning, and he hoped I could quickly visit with an agreement to cement the deal. I was there the next morning.

There are usually options to any proposition. You have to dig for details of what the objections are to be able to propose an option. The quality of the option you propose can be the glue that seals a deal.

Trade-Off

A trade-off is a conditional compromise of positions—if you will give to me, then I will give to you. This tactic is more common in multifaceted negotiations, like those involving labor contracts, than it is in sales. However, you may have an opportunity to use the tactic. Here's an example. You have the good fortune to be the only landscaper that the prospect wants to use for the work in question. Maybe it's because the prospect just doesn't have time to explore other options, or maybe it is because you are so uniquely qualified or equipped for the job. You often put an advertising sign at work locations to promote your business while the work is in progress and for two weeks after that. The prospect has absolutely refused to allow it. You also want two weeks to do the work. The prospect is pushing for one week but has not said absolutely not. The prospect said no to the sign because he just does not want an advertising sign on his property. You know that. You want an extra week to complete the work. So you offer a trade-off. You will drop the demand for a sign, if the prospect will agree to extend the one week deadline to two weeks. You know that the prospect suffers no angst over the extra time, while he really dislikes the idea of the a sign on his lawn. You have helped him select the lesser of two dislikes. In doing so you fit the job into a timeframe that works for you by giving up something (a lawn ad) that might even get you a client. That is a very advantageous trade-off.

Earlier I mentioned the federal debt level increase negotiations. There was a trade-off offered in that process. Both sides wanted deficit reduction as part of the deal. Cutting expenses was a clear path to that goal. One side wanted deep cuts in social services; the other side did not, so it offered moderate cuts in social services for a tax increase for people making over $250,000 annually. However, the first side was opposed to any tax increases, so the trade-off did not work. That happens sometimes. Trade-offs are a tactic that works only when the trade has meaningful value to both parties.

Red Herring

Herring are fish that are a mixed gray and white color. Smoked herring turns reddish in color. In negotiating, a red herring is a demand that has been put up as a smoke screen. It is a demand that you make even though you will not be able to get it. Why would you do that? You do it so you can trade it off.

During the fifteen years I served as the executive director of the American Society of Media Photographers I had to negotiate many deals for corporate sponsorship. One of those deals was for sponsorship of the Society's annual Chapter Presidents Meeting where the fifteen members of the national board of directors and the forty chapter presidents met for three days to coordinate national and local efforts and to adjust policies for a better organization. A major film manufacturer financed 50 percent of the costs of that meeting. The Society paid the other 50 percent. I wanted the entire cost to be underwritten by a sponsor. Coincidently, the film manufacturer sponsor came to me to insist that it wanted a banner at all sessions of the Meeting that read "Partners in Progress." They offered nothing in return. I was asked to give more and get less. That did not work for me. So I approached a competing film manufacturer to see if they had an interest in funding the remaining 50 percent of the meeting. They expressed an interest with no commitment.

I contacted the existing sponsor and said that I would give them the banner if they funded 100 percent of the expenses. They balked loudly. The I told them that I was talking to their competitor about sponsoring the remaining 50 percent of the costs of the meeting. That startled them. I then proposed that, if they would cover 100 percent of the costs, I would stop discussions with their competitor and give them the banner they wanted. I also warned that that, if they did not, I would conclude a deal with their competitor and give them a "Partners in Progress" banner too. I had indirectly offered a trade-off: Exclusive access to national and local leaders with a banner for my removing their competition from the picture. They paid for 100 percent.

The trade-off does not fit neatly into all negotiations, but it fits into some. Recognizing the opportunity is paramount to making a successful trade off.

TINSTAAFL

There Is No Such Thing As A Free Lunch! This mnemonic device helps you to remember the fact that everything has a price of some sort. We have all met a prospect that wanted something for nothing. We have probably all asked for something for nothing at one time or another. I don't know about you, but I generally did not get what I asked for without paying. As a photographer that does assignments for a variety of publications and websites, I am often asked by other parties if I can send them copies of my photos. Of course, they think that because someone has already paid me to take the photographs, I will probably give them away when asked. *Wrong!* I don't do that. In business, you get what you pay for, and you pay for what you get.

I just had that experience two days ago. I had photographed the exterior and interior of a multimillion-dollar house for sale to run as a feature on a news website. The realtor was there when I did the photography. A couple of days later, the photo feature about the house was run on thirteen local websites. The next day, I received an email from the realtor. The exact wording was as follows.

> *Hi Richard,*
>
> *The article and pictures look great! Thanks!*
>
> *Would you be able to send me the pictures to add to a brochure?*
>
> *Will this article run again?*
>
> *Thanks again.*

Here is the answer I sent.

> *I cannot provide the photographs without a fee. Selling real estate is your livelihood; selling photographs is mine. It just does not pay to give away what you sell.*
>
> *If you want them for a brochure I will provide you with high-resolution files. I edited down to twenty-nine photos. I can supply one or all for a brochure. The fee would vary accordingly as I*

> *have to spend time creating the high-resolution*
> *files from the RAW format in which the originals*
> *were shot. However, if you want to entertain the*
> *notion of using me to do real estate photos for it,*
> *I can make a better deal.*

As you can see, I politely told the realtor, "TINSTAAFL," and at the same time I tried to open the door to doing photography work for him. I still have not heard back, so I assume I will not be making that sale or getting work from this person. Fortunately, that does not matter, because I have a successful business that is not dependent upon any one client.

Sometimes I am asked, usually by nonprofit organizations, to donate my services to their cause. On occasion I do it, but rarely. I have an income level that allows me to make a limited number of financial contributions to nonprofit organizations. When I write them a check, I get a tax deduction. If I do photography for them the only thing I can deduct is the cost of the materials, but when I make digital photographs there are few materials used. The value of the time contributed is *not* deductible.

I reply to such requests by saying that I have a number of charities that I support with cash contributions (which are tax deductible). I say that I'll be happy to consider their cause when deciding what contributions to make during the year, but I cannot provide them with free services as I get no tax deduction for something that has a cash value to them and to me. I'd be better off writing a check, because at least I get a tax benefit from it.

Sometimes people do not understand my position. After all, they might be volunteers contributing their time and receiving no tax benefit in return. Basically, they are asking me to become a volunteer for the organization. My reply is that I already volunteer time for several nonprofits, and I have no more free time to give, because I do have to spend most of my time doing paid work to earn a living. I follow up with an offer to give them a special rate. Never miss an opportunity to make a sale.

Positive Priming

You can get people in the habit of saying "yes," which is a word you normally want to hear from your counterpart in a negotiation. The method is really very simple. You ask a series of questions or make a series of statements that will get a positive response in an answer or in the person's mind. It is OK if the person only thinks *yes* without saying it. Here's an example of the kind of progression you can use to get your counterpart to think in the affirmative.

"I have a reputation for not only delivering fine-quality work but also for getting it to my clients on time and within budget. I am sure you want that." Prospect thinks *yes*.

"I assume that your deadline for completion is important as far as timing goes, so an on-time delivery is important." Prospect thinks *yes*.

"Would you feel better if I placed this job a few days sooner in my schedule to assure no delays will interfere with meeting your deadline?" Prospect answers, "Yes."

"I can't promise it, but I assume that if I can bring this job in under budget, you'll be happy." Prospect answers, "Sure will."

"If you can assign this job to me today, I can work it into my schedule very soon. Here's what I have to offer. We can do this job for $5,000. We'll have it wrapped up in two days. Do you want us to start on Tuesday or Wednesday?"

Notice that the last question cannot be answered with a "yes" or a "no." I assume that I have the prospect thinking in positives, that I have the job, and that only the details remain to be pinned down. First, I established a positive line of thought, and then I asked two "yes" questions. Finally, I assumed that I would be doing the job and asked what day they would like me to start work. I don't just ask, "Do I have the job?" Make the assumption that you have it. Don't ask a question that can get a *no* for an answer.

Funny Money

Prospects sometimes make offers of payment that are ridiculously low. This either comes from ignorance of the true value of what you do or is a simple attempt to get you to work cheap. There is a way to deal with this type of situation without being so crass as to say something like "You must be joking." I call the tactic "Funny Money," because it is a rebuttal to a laughable offer.

I get laughable offers regularly. For some reason many people think that photography is easy and inexpensive. Last winter I was asked by the communication director of a local university to photograph an ice hockey game. In his email he wrote that since the game was only an hour long, he thought $100 was a fair fee. This is how I replied.

> *Thank for the offer to work for you. Unfortunately, I cannot accept the work at the fee you have offered. Here is what that fee means in terms of an assignment like the ice hockey game you want me to shoot.*
>
> *Travel time round trip: 1.0 hour*
> *Time on location: 2.0 hours*
> *Editing/image processing: 2.0 hours*
> *Caption photos: .5 hours*
> *Prepare for delivery on disk: .5 hours*

The job is six hours total. For a $100 fee, that comes to $16.67 an hour. If you consider my direct and indirect costs, such as insurance, equipment depreciation, and auto expenses, I will only net about 60 percent of the fee, or $60. After I pay taxes on that $60 it has a value to me of a little over $40. Divide that by the six hours and you find that I would actually be earning less than $7 per hour. Minimum wage in Pennsylvania is $7.25 an hour, and most people who live on minimum wage do not have to pay any income tax.

To illustrate my costs, consider the fact that auto mileage at the 2010 IRS rate is 50 cents per mile, which barely covers the operating costs of an average car with gas prices as high as they are. The game is eighteen miles from my house, making for a roundtrip of thirty-six miles, which would cost $18 in gas. Next is the equipment depreciation. To do what I do at the quality level at which I do it requires that I have nearly $9,000 in pro equipment. That gear has a life of about 5 years, so it is depreciated at the rate of 20 percent or $1,800 per year. I have to make that $1,800 so that I can replace equipment as it wears out or becomes obsolete. I do about 130 assignments a year, so each has to absorb depreciation of nearly $14. This means that gas and equipment depreciation alone would total $32 for this particular job, and that figure reduces the $100 fee offered to an actual value to me of $68. Allow for insurance and taxes and you can see that $40 value to me is not far fetched.

I could not afford to stay in business if I accepted fees in the range you have offered, and if you held to that price you would be forced to work with photographers of lesser quality and experience who might not have the equipment to do your work correctly. In the long run, it is better for your organization to pay more to ensure the quality of supply it needs. Bad photos reflect bad communications, which in turn reflect poorly on the institution using them. In a world in which we are deluged with images, only the best quality stands out.

I can accept your assignment for a fee of $300. I hope to hear from you soon, as I book up dates fast at this time of year.

When you are given a laughable offer don't laugh. Instead break the payment down to understandable units of time and costs to show the prospect how the money doesn't warrant the time and effort involved. Always be prepared to present just how laughable an offer is by offering a detailed analysis with no laughter.

Flinching

This tactic is often combined with the Bold Response tactic previously described. It should be used sparingly, because it can startle your counterpart. Of course, there are times when you *need* to startle them. A flinch is a visual cue intended to provide a clue. For example, picture yourself sitting across a table across from your counterpart with your hands folded and resting on the table in front of you. The client makes a ridiculous demand. You respond visually by pulling your hands up off the table and separating them, and then by placing them back on the table and lightly grasping its edge. At the same time you exclaim in a firm (not loud) voice, "That's totally unacceptable. I am going to have to pay that much to my helper on this job. I can't afford to work for my helper's wages. I'm long past that level of experience."

You rejected the offer with a bold and candid response, while at the same time reinforcing your message with a gesture of dislike, i.e., a flinch. The table-grasping gesture was a body language message that showed that you went from interested (folded hands) to uninterested (hands grasping), thereby reinforcing your Bold Response.

A flinch can be more dramatic, and again I advise that drama has a place in a negotiation only when all else is failing. Here is another true-life example from a negotiation in which I was defending the copyright rights of photographers. In 1990, an amendment to the federal copyright law was introduced in the Senate. The amendment, know as the Visual Artists Rights Act, would provide certain protections to the creators of fine art. In defining "fine art," the drafter of the legislation omitted photography as a class of fine art. Acting in my capacity as executive director of the American Society of Media Photographers, I went to Capitol Hill and visited with the drafters, who acknowledged the omission as an oversight and quickly corrected the omission. Job done. No negotiation required.

A few months later, I learned that photography was likely to be dropped from the final legislation. Another visit with a senatorial staffer was in order. During that meeting I opened with my favorite question: Why? I was calmly sitting there, speaking in a normal tone of voice. The reply to my question was "Because publishers say they will have the bill defeated if we keep photography in it." Understand this: Magazine and book publishers were going have a bill about fine artists rights defeated because some of the photographers they published were fine artists.

Instantly, I knew a forceful reaction was called for to make the people across the table understand that their decision to drop photography from the bill was unacceptable. I stood up, put my hands on the table, leaned in toward them, and in a forceful voice said, "If you drop photography from the legislation, I will put together a coalition of artists' organizations that will oppose the bill. We'll come to the hearings and explain that we do not want a law that discriminates against one class of creator. Don't you think that all creators, just like individuals, are created equal?" Then I sat back down and waited for an answer.

The answer was that they really wanted to get this protection for artists, so keeping the publishers from opposing the bill was critical. I asked what the publishers feared. The answer was an enumeration of several points that I knew could be worked out as long as I kept the pressure on. I replied with something like "I really do not want to kill the legislation, so I hope you don't make me do it. Here are some possible options in the bill's provisions that ought to alleviate the publishers' concerns. Please take them to the publishers, and if they are interested in talking, let me know when. I am headed back to my office to start calling artists' organizations. I hope to hear from you soon." I left.

In the end, we reached a compromise with the publishers, and the legislation passed in both the Senate and House. Did my exaggerated flinch have some effect on the conclusion? I can't know for sure, but I do know this: I had to impress them with the level of my disappointment and make them believe that I was so outraged that I would carry out my threat to organize a coalition to defeat the legislation. It is very unlikely that I could have ever organized a coalition, because organizations do not oppose legislation that is good for their members, even if it is not good for others. However, I had to make the senatorial staffers believe I would do it. They did not want to take that risk, so they went back to the publishers even though those publishers were big campaign contributors. Sometimes you just have to be very forceful.

Limited Authority

In some business circles limited authority is becoming a way of life rather than an occasional tactic. When your negotiating counterpart does not have the authority to make a deal, his authority is limited. He is a messenger to the person who has the proper level of authority. He takes your offer to someone else who decides on it. If it is refused, as it often is, you have to rework your offer and present it again. It is a way to force your position downward. It is not a good position to be in and ought to be avoided. To find out if a person has limited authority, just ask if he is empowered to approve and to sign-off on the deal.

When I am not certain of a person's level of authority I always ask: "If we can reach an agreement, are you authorized to sign off on it?" If they say no, I ask who has that authority and whether I can meet with that person. You should always ask to meet the person with authority, because only you can convey your message the way you want it conveyed. However, you probably won't get what you ask for. In that case, you should make your offer conditional by reserving the right to change it or withdraw it at any time. My usual way of saying it is: "Since you do not have the authority to sign off on a deal I have to reserve the right to change any offer I make. I have to do that because a lot can be lost when a messenger conveys my offer to another person." That way you are negotiating on the same ground: you have not made a solid commitment in any offer you put forward. If your offer is rejected and more is asked for, you can rearrange your entire offer at will. Using limited authority seems like game playing to me. I don't play games when I negotiate, and you should not either.

Good Cop/Bad Cop

If you have ever seen a detective film with an interrogation scene in it, you have most likely seen the tactic when one cop leans hard on the suspect trying to break him, and then another cop eventually steps in and "rescues" the suspect from the hard-line treatment.

This is a tactic that is used by buyers on occasion. You have probably experienced the negotiating situation in which your counterpart blames something you don't like on another person. They are saying that they have limited authority as I described in the previous section, and the person with the authority is the bad guy. Often it's the lawyer or accountant who insisted that they make such a demand. The good guy is talking to you and the bad guy is leaning on you. Of course the bad guy isn't present. In such a situation you ought to insist on talking with the bad guy. You cannot negotiate without one of the players involved. Negotiating with a messenger is as inefficient as negotiating can get. The messenger has no power. He is only a mouthpiece. Mouths may speak agreements, but brains decide them. You want the brains in the room.

Good cop/bad cop is also a tactic that you can use in some situations, if you have a partner, sales manager, or sales representative. You and that person agree that he should drive the hardest deal possible to condition the client's desire for some relief. Your representative and the buyer reach an impasse, but the job actually does meet your bottom line. Your representative is pushing to get a fee that the client is resisting. He says he has to speak with you to go out of the limits he has offered. After he speaks with you, he comes back to the prospect with "My boss wouldn't normally do this, but we haven't any work with you in the past, and we really want to show you what we can do on a big job like this. The boss has approved the acceptance of the fee you offered this time as a gesture of goodwill."

The boss became the good guy and the tactic was used to avoid the impasse and get the job. One thing you must remember is that both the good guy and the bad guy have to have previously discussed the use of this tactic. The last thing you want to do is surprise each other.

Reverse It

You will recall that one characteristic of good negotiators is that they are empathetic. Empathy is an understanding of the experience of the other party. It should not be confused with sympathy, that is, feeling sorry for the other person. Most reasonable people are empathetic. You can reach out to the empathetic negotiators by asking them to reverse situations in their minds. Ask them to consider what their reaction would be if they were in your place.

An example of reversing can be developed around the example of the Funny Money tactic discussed above. Using that tactic, I pointed out that the true value of the prospect's offer to me was less than half of the fee offered to me. When that happens to you, try to get the prospect to be empathetic. Here is what I could have said in that previous example: "What you are asking me to do is work for less than half of my usual fee. I can't afford to do that. Suppose your boss came to you and asked you to reduce your salary by half while you work on this job. Would you do it? You know you wouldn't, and you shouldn't. The value you bring to the work doesn't change with the work, so your pay should not change either. Well, that is exactly how I feel about my fee for this work. I am sure that you can see it from my point of view, so can we talk about a reasonable fee?"

Appealing to their sense of empathy, you asked your counterpart to imagine the same kind of thing happening to him, and then you asked for fair treatment. It is hard to ask a person to give up what you wouldn't give up yourself. Reverse that on your counterpart and you might just move him closer to your position.

Challenge for a Change

This tactic is nothing more than confronting what is presented as a non-negotiable position. Should you accept the fact that a deal is take-it-or-leave-it, just because someone says it is? No, not until you challenge it. Making a non-negotiable offer is the height of arrogance. It reduces what should be a mutually cooperative relationship to a one-side-gets-all situation.

You can and should resist a non-negotiable offer by challenging it. What you might say is "I think that you are being unfair. Let me ask you a question: Do you think that the best way for two people to make a deal is to make a deal that is fair to both of them?" If the person says yes, he's saying he doesn't believe in fair dealing. In that case you can say: "I'm really surprised, even though I know you think your offer is fair. You're not giving me the opportunity to explain why it doesn't meet my needs—that is, why it is not fair to me. Allow me to explain why that's so, and what it would take to make a deal within the limits that would allow me to do this job. Then we can conduct this meeting knowing we both want to be fair."

Your challenge might be futile. Some people refuse to negotiate. If you can't force a negotiation, then evaluate the deal based on what you're being offered and what your needs are. If the offer meets your bottom-line needs, take it. If it doesn't, leave it. If you can afford to walk away, I recommend doing so. People who refuse to negotiate are likely to be troublesome in the future. Maybe they will come back to you when the job is complete yet unpaid for to complain about something. Now they have your money and control over the situation. Are they about to negotiate the dispute? Not likely. Thy are more likely to put a non-negotiable settlement on the table.

I am offered unfair non-negotiable offers every week. I have the good fortune to not be dependent upon any one client or assignment. I always turn them down unless they are well above my bottom line. A non-negotiable offer at a good price is more appealing than a marginal one. If there is a later dispute, I am confident that I will be able to handle it because I have the experience necessary to do so.

DISARMING INTIMIDATION

Intimidation is a tactic used by some buyers. What do you do when you realize that someone is trying to intimidate you? I can answer that by example.

Years ago, I was doing a great deal of corporate work for different communication departments within a large teaching hospital, such as those in the medical school, the nursing school, the research center, and the hospital itself. One day, I could not resolve a difference in positions with one of the communication directors. I had the experience and the equipment needed to do the work best. I knew I had little, if any, competition. At some point I made it clear that I was not going to lower my price, because I thought it was more than fair in light of the fact that I couldn't think of a soul who was better equipped and qualified to do the job. The communication director didn't like my answer. He said that in that case I was going to lose the job. I acknowledged his words as his decision, and said I was sorry to hear it, but it was his choice, and I respected it. Then came the bombshell. He said that he might feel compelled to tell other departmental communication directors in the hospital about how difficult I had become to work with, and that could cost me more work. My reaction was swift and soft. I calmly said, "I have confidence in two of my beliefs. First, I believe that any communication directors connected with this institution will know that to be false, just as you know it to be false. Second, I believe that since you know what you said is not true, and since you are a decent person, you would never do such a thing."

He immediately apologized and offered that the stress of the past days had gotten to him, suggesting that we pick up the next day to see if we could resolve the matter. What I had done was reject his intimidation attempt, explain why, and excuse him. He knew I wasn't going to be intimidated, and I didn't have to make threats to protect myself.

Suppose he had responded to my polite rebuttal by telling me that he had every intention of carrying out his threat. I would have told him that I was going to put the hospital's legal department on notice that he was threatening to blackball me in order to intimidate me into dropping my price—and that, if he ever did blackball me, the hospital could expect to hear from my lawyer. I would also refuse to quote any more jobs for him, to prove that I was not simply bluffing. I would also have made it clear that he had better be sure that all the other communication directors liked him better than they liked me, because it would only take *one* of them to back up my fitness for the work and the fairness of my prices, and that would put him in real hot water for making an illegal threat. The reason I would do these things is simple: I do not succumb to threats. Who needs a client like him? Never submit to intimidation.

Avoid a Liar

Fortunately, it is a rare situation to encounter a liar in a negotiation. When I speak of a liar I am not referring to a person who occasionally uses an inconsequential lie, sometimes called a white lie. I am talking about the liar who will truly deceive you to get his way.

Unfortunately, you rarely find out that you have been deceived before it is too late. In some situations, you might be able to take action if the lie ends up costing you something of value—like money or reputation. However, the probability of taking a loss can be decreased. When you are negotiating you must keep good notes of what is being said and of agreements made. Doing so protects your interests. When I see people discussing business and not taking notes, I am always shocked. Either they are sloppy, or they have exceptional memories and are just foolish.

Taking notes of the discussion and outcomes can be the path to resolving later disputes over the deal when the work is underway or done. When you are making a deal with a previously unknown person you do not know whether they are capable of lying to you. Why take a chance? It is better to protect yourself, and you can do that by taking notes. I do it all the time. When the deal is made I read back my notes to the other person, and I ask them if they agree with what I have just said. If they don't agree, we have to review the parts of the deal that cause disagreement. If they do agree then I note it, and consider it a level of proof that the notes reflect the deal made. There is more.

By reading back my notes I let the other party know that I am keeping a record of what is being said and agreed to. By asking them to approve the representations in my notes I have some way to defend myself against a person who has lied to me in a negotiation and subsequently does not keep his end of the deal.

Finally, if you have been lied to before by the same person you are negotiating with currently, you must be crazy or reckless. Remember that old adage: "Fool me once, shame on you. Fool me twice, shame on me." How true! The only defense is to avoid him. Just as you would fire a dishonest employee, you should "fire" a dishonest buyer or seller by refusing to do business with him.

The accomplished liar can always get the best of you, because he not only does not strive to be fair, but he is also intentionally unfair. If they lied about the deal, they will probably lie about anything if it gives them an advantage. Once you know a person to be a liar the only defense is to avoid him. Just as you would fire a dishonest employee, you should "fire" a dishonest person by refusing to do business with him.

Missing Links

There are two reasons people fail to negotiate deals that are better than the ones they are first offered: 1) failure to formulate a negotiating strategy, and 2) ignorance of negotiating tactics. Photographers who fail to get better deals often say that their prospects won't negotiate. What they are often really saying is that they failed to begin a negotiation because they failed to think about negotiating or failed to learn how to negotiate.

By developing a negotiating strategy you take the first step toward initiating negotiations. That first step gives you a direction, an approach, and a goal for the negotiating process. Once the negotiation begins in earnest, the wide variety of tactics available to you enables you to present and promote your position, while moving your counterpart closer to your position. Don't have any missing links in your business efforts. Failure to negotiate is a missing link, and a missing link means the chain is broken.

Chapter Six

NEGOTIATING CONTRACTS

Y ou can't be in business without sooner or later being handed a contract to sign. It might be a contract to purchase goods or services or, even more likely, to provide them. Regardless of which, there is never any reason to assume that a contract is ready to be signed the second it is presented for your signature. In spite of that fact, many business people are all too ready to sign on the bottom line without critically examining the contract, discussing its terms, and negotiating those terms to arrive at a more acceptable agreement. There seems to be an instinctive belief that a contract is a take-it-or-leave-it offer, and no negotiation is possible. The simple fact is that there are few contracts written that are not negotiable. The few that do exist are usually products of a negotiation that preceded the drafting of the contract. So let's learn how to negotiate a contract, so that you have a say in the agreement.

REQUIRED EXPERTISE

Developing expertise in contract negotiating takes four things. First, you have to know what a contract is and is not. Expertise means specific knowledge, and you get that by study. Second, you have to have an understanding of language. You do not have to have the word skills of a writer, let alone a lawyer, but you do have to have a reasonable grasp of contract language. If you don't have that, then get help before you try to negotiate. Third, you have to know the tactical means of negotiating. By that I mean how to explain why your counterpart's demands are unacceptable and how to offer alternatives that are acceptable. If all you do is reject without offering alternatives, you are simply refusing and not negotiating. Fourth, you have to learn to keep the process in perspective. Contracts are not enforceable until the parties sign them. There is no liability in negotiating. There may be some if you do not.

WHAT IS A CONTRACT?

From a business perspective, a contract is a mutual understanding. Legally, a contract is an enforceable agreement. "Enforceable" is the keyword. We can enter into many agreements in life, but most of them are not enforceable.

Here's an example. A client asks you to do some work for him. His budget is low, and your price is high. He asks you for a price reduction on the work, and he says that he will make it up to you on the next job you do for him. You agree and give him the discounted price that he is looking for. A few weeks go by and he calls you with the next job he has. Does he have to provide you with that extra payment he promised? No, he does not, because the agreement that you made with him is not an enforceable agreement. In short, it is not a contract. All your client did was to promise you a better deal. You accepted the promise. Both of you agreed, but you did not form a contract. He made you an offer, and you accepted it, but the deal lacked one critical component, consideration. Consideration is something of value that the parties exchange to support the offer and acceptance made in the course of the deal. Both of you agreed, but you did not form a contract. A contract must have three things: offer, acceptance, and consideration. When all three are present there is an enforceable agreement, a contract, on the table.

CONTRACT TYPES

Contracts can be either written or spoken. Spoken contracts are sometimes referred to as "verbal" or "oral." Let's call the spoken contract "oral," since all contracts consist of words (the meaning of "verbal"). While the principles of negotiating are applied to both written and oral contracts, if you are going to go to the trouble of negotiating a contract, you ought to have it written down when you are done. Poor recollection of oral-contract terms have probably led to more avoidable business disputes than any other cause. Avoid oral agreements in business. They are generally worthless in any subsequent dispute. That is why your client often presents you with a contract to sign when offering you work.

INITIAL STEPS

Negotiating a contract requires three important initial steps. Skipping any one of these is almost a guarantee of failure. When you receive a contract it is wise to make at least one photocopy of it. This is an editing copy. It allows you to mark up the contract with notes, cross outs, and additions without making the original unusable. Once that is done, you are ready to take the first three steps.

Read It

Step one is reading the proposed contract. I say proposed because it is not a contract until you agree to it. You are reading an offer from your client. Keep that mind-set. It is an offer, not a decree. As you read the document, make pencil notes on your photocopy. A few key words to jog your memory on what came to mind as you read each section will usually do. You can use a yellow highlighter to mark the parts that you know you will want to negotiate. Usually, those deal with fees, rights, and liability. Underline in red any word that you do not understand. There are many words in the dictionary; if the person who drafted the contract used words that you do not understand, you cannot have a "mutual understanding" until you understand those words.

Keep a dictionary at hand. Look up any word for which you do not have clear understanding of the meaning. Misinterpretation of the meaning of a word can often lead to future problems, and sometimes those problems end up in the courtroom at great expense to the parties. One example of how a definition can mean so much can be demonstrated by the word "advertising." A photographer signed a contract granting "advertising rights" to a client. The client placed ads in magazines and printed brochures to sell its product. The photographer protested the brochure use, claiming it to be promotional, not advertising, use. The case went to court. The photographer lost the case. The judge relied on the dictionary definition of the word "advertising," which is "the act of calling something to the public's attention." The judge said that the magazine ads and the brochures fit the definition perfectly. The judge rejected the photographer's argument that photographers had a different understanding of the word. He said people rely on dictionaries for meanings and not on photographers' interpretations. The lesson learned is to keep a dictionary nearby. A broadly defined word is exactly that. If you don't want to accept broad interpretations, then don't accept broadly defined words. Specifics are better than generalities in contracts.

Understand the Content

Once you have edited the contract you are ready to move on to step two. First, write down any words that are underlined in red. Then write the dictionary definition of the word next to it. You will refer to this list later on. Review your editing copy and make a list of each problematic clause in the same order as these clauses appear in the contract. These should be highlighted in yellow and easy to find. Then think about possible alternatives to the clauses that you have listed. Maybe it means adding some words or deleting others. You might have to rewrite an entire clause. In the end, you should have a clause that you want to substitute in place of the one offered. These newly constructed clauses will be your counteroffer. Make sure that you have those new clauses spelled out exactly, word for word. You do not want to be formulating your position in your head in the middle of the negotiation (unless you must).

Now make some notes about why you can't accept the clause or clauses as offered. A good negotiator has a reason for rejecting any word, clause, or contract, and at the same time has an alternative to offer. As a final process in this step you should also write down the minimum you will accept— that is, the bottom line for each of the clauses in dispute. If you have no bottom line, there was no reason to begin the negotiation. Having no bottom line means that, eventually, you will probably accept the offer as made to you in the first place.

Reach Agreement

So far, you have evaluated the offering and come up with a counteroffer. Now it is time to move on to step three: reaching agreement. It is time to talk to your counterpart. Simple negotiations can often be handled with a brief phone call. Complex ones often require an exchange of written drafts, along with phone calls to discuss the reasoning behind positions. Note that I said "reasoning." Negotiation is more about reasons that make sense than it is about power. You should never do something that does not make sense to you. Nor should your counterpart. A meeting of the minds results in a mutual understanding only when the parties are reasonable. You cannot negotiate with an unreasonable party, and there are such people and companies. The most difficult negotiations are best handled face to face when the situation permits, because most people want to be "seen" as reasonable.

EASIER TO HARDER

Resolve the least-disputed clauses first. This sets a tone for future agreement, and the word "yes" is easier to get if it is part of a pattern of "yeses." Prove that the two of you can agree on the easy ones, so it will be easier to reach agreement on the difficult ones. The added benefit of working from easier to harder issues is that once both sides have committed time and energy to resolving some of the issues, it is harder for both to give up on a tough issue because of that time and energy investment. Compromises on the difficult issues are simply more acceptable when you have already made good progress to that point.

TACTICAL CONSIDERATIONS

The tactics used in negotiating contracts are no different than those used to negotiate an assignment or a stock photography sale. The trial balloon and the trade-off are probably two of the most used tactics in contract negotiations. You offer alternatives on a hypothetical basis; and you give in on one clause or part thereof to get the other side to give in on another. Every tactic you read about earlier in this book applies when negotiating a contract.

EXPERTISE

When you are dealing with a contract, don't make the mistakes of either thinking that you have legal expertise, or that all legal expertise on the other side is correct. Lawyers make mistakes just as photographers do. When you are confronted with a legal concern in a contract, like a liability or hold-harmless clause, you should have someone with proven expertise check the clause. What's the difference between negligence, gross negligence, and willful negligence? I am not asking what you think the words mean: I am asking how the legal system decides which exists. A lawyer, not you or I, should answer that question.

Here's another example. Most contracts have an indemnification or hold-harmless clause. When you are indemnified—that is, when the other side will pay any losses you incur from any claim made against you—will the indemnifier pay for your defense if you are sued, or just pay the judgment against you? It will pay for your defense, if you add the words "and provide a defense for" immediately after the word "indemnify." Once again, a lawyer will pick up such things in a contract's legal provisions.

Contracts can have business issues and/or legal issues. Legal issues are best either handled by a lawyer or, if handled by you, with a lawyer's counsel. It is easier for a lawyer to make good photographs than it is for a photographer to practice law capably. A little money spent on a lawyer as preventive medicine can eliminate the huge expense of hiring a lawyer to fight the lawsuit that arises because you either didn't understand the contract or didn't understand your legal obligations under the contract you signed.

A good friend of mine has been a lawyer for decades. He describes some lawyers as "deal breakers." He means that once they are called in, they make it a point to find so many things wrong with a deal waiting to be finalized that the contract falls apart. Please do not take this to be a condemnation of lawyers. I think lawyers are indispensable when it comes to protecting a business. I don't think that they are indispensable when it comes to running a business. Business persons run businesses. Lawyers practice law. When you need legal advice on a contract's legalities get it, but make your own decisions about the business aspects.

Wrapping Up

You can now see that, with the exception of the legal aspects of contracts, the process of negotiating a contract goes through the same stages and uses the same tactics as any other negotiation. Your homework is reading and understanding the contract, coupled with evaluating the issues and constructing alternatives to things you have problems with. Discussions employ traditional tactics, and eventually you end up with an agreement; or you don't agree and there will be no contract. Some elements of the contract might require consulting a lawyer, who you ought to select for his legal expertise, not because he has lots of opinions about how you should run your business.

The wrap up to negotiating a contract is signing it, the simplest act in the process.

Chapter Seven

NEGOTIATING THE SERVICE DEAL

O f all the negotiating challenges a business person encounters, negotiating a deal for services is usually the most difficult. I am not saying it is difficult by nature. I am saying that the negotiation of a deal for services is more difficult when compared to negotiating a sale of goods. The reason I say this is because you are negotiating a price for something that does not exist at the time of the negotiation. You are negotiating for the opportunity to make something exist. Unlike a sale or purchase of goods, the tangible product of services rendered does not exist until the job is done. In other words, the buyer does not know exactly what he is buying. Buyer uncertainty can result in extreme caution being taken. The buyer is often more inclined to seek a low price thinking that it protects his interests if something turns out poorly. A good negotiator know he has to deal with buyer uncertainty.

FEAR OF THE INTANGIBLE

Take a moment to think about buying shares of stock in a corporation. You are buying a piece of paper that has an assigned value on the day you buy it. This value is based upon many factors, including the emotion-driven, fickle stock markets of the world. You could pay $100 per share for a stock on Monday, and it could drop in value by 50 percent by Friday. While you hope that your research into the company whose stock you are buying will protect your investment, you realize that there are factors beyond your control that can affect the value of any stock shares that you buy. One major factor is the performance of the company issuing the stock.

Likewise, the outcome of a service rendered is dependent upon the performance of the provider. A complex service may also be dependent upon the performance of several other people under the prime provider's control: subcontractors, suppliers, preparers, and others might be involved in making a job a success. The buyer is taking a risk based upon your company's performance. That makes performance an issue.

PERFORMANCE ISSUES

Place yourself in a buyer's shoes for moment. A person is planning a house addition with a budget of $50,000. Much work has to be done before that addition will be ready for use. Some of that work has to be done before the actual fabrication begins, because plans have to be drawn. The architect selected will charge a fee of $5,000. That fact increases pressure on the buyer and can make him very concerned about the outcome. The buyer's concern is that the plans have to conform to the budget, that is, those plans cannot result in construction costs in excess of $45,000 (the budget less the architect's fee). Until the architect's plans are seen by the builder, no estimate of construction costs is possible. The buyer will be dependent upon the architect's performance in terms of his ability to create designs and specifications that fit within the budget minus his fee.

Now assume you are the architect and you have to assure the buyer that you will meet his needs. If you reflect on the previous chapter, you will recall that these performance issues are to be considered in the strategy formulation for your negotiation. You will also recall that some tactics are natural fits for performance issues. Tactical commitment—that is, offering proof that you can meet all the performance demands of the work to be done—is a natural fit for dealing with performance issues. It should be included as part of your sales pitch in any attempt to secure an assignment when the client is not aware, from personal experience, of your ability to perform. Remember, every architect seeking the assignment will show a prospective buyer a list of happy clients. However, that list does not speak to performance in a totally convincing manner; after all, who knows which of those architect's clients had similar budget limitations that were met?

A list of satisfied clients with contacts and phone numbers is a great testimony to your performance. If that list indicates satisfied clients that were in a budgeting situation similar to the buyer of the house addition, it is more reassuring. The mere fact that you offer such a list demonstrates that you have confidence in your performance. Confidence is contagious—help your client catch it. Deal with performance issues head-on and set the prospect's mind more at ease than your competition will. When you do this, you will have positioned yourself for a successful negotiation of the remaining bargaining issues.

Finally, it never hurts to replay your message about your performance capability. Mentioning your commitment to performance at critical stages when dealing with the value issues—without being a broken record—can only help you in the client's mind.

Value Issues

In addition to the performance issues mentioned above, you need to focus on value issues. The four main value issues in a negotiation for services are time, materials, overhead, and timing. Time and materials are highly recognized parts of pricing we always consider. Overhead has a value too and you can find it in your P&L as indirect expenses. However, one value item that is often overlooked is time versus timing. That will be discussed below.

What this book does not cover is how to arrive at the value of your time, expenses, and overhead. Those are business matters and are outside the scope of this book. If you need to learn more about arriving at appropriate value for these items, you might want to find a good book about basic business.

Time and Timing

You have undoubtedly heard the saying "Time is money." In business, that is a true equation. Another true thing about time is that it is the only thing you are sure to eventually and permanently run out of. That makes it extremely valuable. You charge a fee for your time. That fee is negotiable, as it should be. Your negotiating success will set the value of your time. It's that simple when it comes to time that you are selling. However, there is another aspect involved in determining the value of time in a negotiation: Some time is more valuable than other time. Let me explain.

There are some days in everyone's working schedule when the workload is lighter than at other times. If you can shift your workload from one time to another, it can mean that your earnings will increase. An example of this concept follows.

You are called to provide a quote for services to be performed on a certain day, let's say a Tuesday. It happens that you are already committed on that Tuesday. That means you lose the job unless you can shift the day that one of the jobs is done. It is difficult, and may be unwise, to postpone scheduled work. Clients generally do not like to change schedules, and postponing work in order to do another job for a different client is like telling the original client that his work is not as important to you. A more successful approach would be to time-shift the work of the prospect who is offering the new job. Shifting the time will allow you to make money that you would otherwise not receive. You might consider proposing a discounted fee if the job being offered can be shifted to a different day. This does not mean that you should discount the overhead or materials; that would be like throwing away your money. Time-shifting is all about getting money that you might otherwise not receive. A slight reduction in the value of your time could result in timing that lands the job on your to-do list.

Time-shifting usually comes into play on smaller, routine jobs. Big productions usually have to be planned well in advance, so they are normally scheduled for available days.

Less complicated jobs are more likely candidates for time-shifting. These are jobs that don't usually require that you spend lots of time calculating the price. You routinely know what you charge for them. So you can give a price early and quickly.

Offering a time-shift discount is simple to do. You simply discount the time by any amount you feel is worth giving up to get the extra revenues. You put your price on the table with a condition. You might say it this way: "Normally I would charge $1,000 for this job, but if you can shift it from Tuesday to another day, I can do it for $900. I am so jammed up on Tuesday that it's worth it to me to discount my price to shift the work. In fact, if it can't be shifted from Tuesday, I'd better pass on it. I can't ask my other client to postpone. I don't want to inconvenience them. What do you say? What other day do you want me to shoot the job?"

You have just offered a conditional discount as an incentive, and you have reinforced your commitment to the welfare of your clients by not inconveniencing one with a change of shooting date. Buyers like discounts, and they like suppliers who protect their interests. You have provided a *practical* advantage in a discount and a *psychological* advantage in shaping the client's positive impression of you.

PROFESSIONAL FEE NEGOTIATIONS

Negotiating a professional fee for intangible work products is always the hardest task in a selling situation. The reason for this is that professionals do not have an industry-wide pricing method or standard for pricing services performed. It is impossible to price creativity or expertise by formula. You know your overhead, but how do you put a price tag on the creativity and experience that you bring to a job? You can't—at least you can't do it before the job is done. After it is over, you know, or at least have a good feel for, the level of creative energy that went into the work, but can you really put a price tag on it? I don't think you can, and neither can your prospect or client. You know that some jobs require more creativity than others. For example, preparation of an agreement of sale for real estate is basic legal work, but how much special insight does it take? It takes some, but not as much as much as writing a contract to build a shopping center.

The fact is that much work that professionals do requires careful craftsmanship, but it doesn't require great expertise. While most professionals will try to be more innovative, there is often little room to introduce highly innovative thinking into work products because either time or circumstances do not allow it. This means that you have to distinguish between what I call the "bread and butter" jobs and the "champagne" jobs. Most businesses run on "bread and butter" jobs, and they get a real boost in monetary and psychic income from the occasional "champagne" job. The first thing you have to distinguish before you offer or negotiate your fee is which kind of job are you being considered for. You will have more serious competition for the "bread and butter" job, and that means that you have to be more conservative in pricing it. Jobs requiring exceptional creativity and/or experience will usually have fewer qualified bidders, and while competition could be fierce, being part of a smaller pool of suppliers usually means that you can be a bit less conservative in pricing.

FEE SETTING

Decide your fee on the basis of the level of experience, capability, and talent that the job really requires, and how much better you are than your competition when it comes to the kind of work you are being asked to do. If your price is questioned or challenged use those factors to sell the fee. You can point to other work of a similar nature—whether done for the same client or a different one—to demonstrate that you received a fee similar to the one you are quoting for the present job. Give examples of the similar work that was similarly paid. It is your responsibility to justify your fee. Do it with facts and common sense. Quality includes completing the job on time, within the quoted price, and in an innovative manner when possible. That is what you are pricing. Anyone can deliver a work product that meets the prospect's basic needs, but you are going to deliver a result that meets the prospect's wants. This is more about selling than about negotiation. It is a good time to be a "broken record." Be direct and confident. Reassert that your fee is reasonable and your services are superior.

Ask About the Fee

If your client cannot accept your fee offer, then try asking a question like "Based upon your experience, what do you think the fee should be?" If the client's answer is close to yours, you can compromise. If it is not, you have a problem, and you have to ask the client if he really wants to work with you specifically. You cannot cut your fee by a substantial amount. If you do, you have told the client that you were just trying to exploit him with your first offer. The job cannot be worth $5,000 when you initially present the price and $4,000 a few minutes later. That is like saying that you padded the estimate by 25 percent. Do you want to work with people who pad their estimates to you?

There is no such thing as the correct fee. If anyone knew the correct fee for all professional work, he would be indispensable, famous, and wealthy. Fee negotiation requires balancing interests: yours, your client's, and. in the case of an intermediary, their client. Your fee has to reflect the value of what you do for the client while preserving the value of what you bring to the job. Value is relative to the experience, creativity, capability, and reliability that you bring to the job, and it is relative to other costs the client will incur in the project. When a company is doing a very expensive project, it is not looking for the cheapest professional around because it is investing in the project for a return. Keep that in mind. Tell prospects that, if they want to maximize their investment, the best way they can do it is by maximizing the quality of the work they buy, and that means that you are the right person for the job, and that the right person costs more than the wrong person.

Always keep in mind when closing a sale that what you do has value. If it did not, the client would not be trying to buy it. You know the value of your services. The client might not agree with you. If you can develop a good rapport with your client, you might be able to get him to share her insights into the value of a job with you. That is not easily done, and it usually requires that you have some kind of ongoing relationship with the client. However, your value increases as your rapport with the person does. When a person convincingly tells you that she wants you to do the work, but that the fee cannot be more than a given amount, you have achieved some level of rapport. You have convinced the client of your value and gotten the admission that he cannot afford your price. It is up to you to decide whether to meet his needs. Maybe you can do it with a reasonable rationale for lowering your price. Reasons like I want to show you what I can do, or because you are such a good client, are acceptable reasons to lower a fee, but not to take a loss. Some differences of opinion cannot be resolved. Sometimes you have to say no. Remember, no one ever went out of business by saying no to a bad deal. Many people have gone out of business by saying yes to bad deals. Stay out of the latter group. Know your value and don't work for less, unless you are sure that it is a one-time step to achieving greater value in the future.

The Bottom Line

Just as the bottom line of a financial statement is the ultimate result, the bottom line in a negotiation the ultimate outcome below which you cannot concede. You must have a bottom line when it comes to fees. That bottom line should be based upon the costs of operating your business. You have to receive a certain level of income just to stay in business. Your financial management planning effort should have produced that number. It takes a certain number of jobs to reach that level of income. Each job has to produce revenues that when all related direct and indirect costs are deducted does not result in a loss. When a job doesn't measure up to that level, you ought to pass on it. If it does, you have a reason to take it.

I once met a fellow who said he didn't mind taking a loss on a job because he could make it up on another job. I asked if he thought is fair to overcharge one client to pay the loss incurred with another client. He thought that was OK. Well, it is not OK for several reasons. First, business logic dictates that your business be profitable. It defies common sense to knowingly plan to take a loss. Second, client A should not be paying for part of client B's work. Would you knowingly pay a vendor to make it possible for him to work for a loss on another job? I would not, and I doubt that you would either.

OPTIONS PACKAGE

Over the years, I learned that almost any fee I placed on the table was going to be too high in the prospect's mind. If a prospect accepted my proposed fee without any discussion, I knew that I had priced the work too low. I hated that feeling. Fortunately, I managed to avoid that experience and find a way to focus fee negotiations quickly and usually in my favor. You and your prospect have positions on price. That sets up a negotiating range—with your position on fee at the top end of the range and his position at the bottom of the range. You normally end up somewhere in between the two opposing starting positions. However, your deal will also have likely terms and conditions like deadlines, deposits, expense reimbursements, insurance requirements, etc. Those things play a part in a complex negotiation. A good negotiator tries to connect all those dots in a packaged deal. Here's an example from my business.

I developed a way to set up a negotiating range that made my job easier. I combined the fee, terms and conditions into a package, and then I proposed it along with two alternative packages. Each package had its own specific grant of rights and specific fee. In other words, I would offer a menu with three options. By doing that, I pushed the negotiation toward considering my range of offers rather than the range set up by my prospect's and my positions on price alone. The three options offered a range fees that went from my wants to my needs and a range of rights that were similarly arranged.

To understand the following example you need to know that in high-end commercial photography the price paid by a client is composed of production costs and a fee based upon how the work product will be used. For example, a photograph reproduced to fill a one-quarter page costs less than a half page. A license for an annual report costs more than a license for a newspaper article. With that understanding in mind you will see from the following example how to set up a negotiating range of your construction.

An Options Example

My prospect is asking for me to quote a price for photography for an annual report and he wants all rights (the right to do anything he wants with the images at any time). He has indicated a willingness to pay $10,000 plus expenses. Some of the images will be generic and will have value as stock photography (photographs that can be used in applications other than the immediate client's). Some of the images will be proprietary, and I will have to protect them from use by anyone other than my client. It will take five days on location to shoot and another five days for travel and pre- and postproduction. My usual rate for this kind of work is $1,000 per day but that does not include "all rights." Normally I double my fee when I have to surrender "all rights." That means I want a $20,000 fee to fulfill the client's wants. Note we are talking about "wants," not needs.

I know that most annual report images will not be used for more than one year. There are some exceptions to this. For example, executive portraits might be re-used for the next year's annual report. They also will likely be used whenever the client needs an executive portrait to send out for publicity uses. I also know that some of the photographs are likely to end up in a corporate brochure or press releases within the next two years, because annual-report photographs often make good material for such collateral uses. That means that the client's needs are one year of use in the annual report, collateral use of the images for two years, and continuing use of the executive portraits.

The client's negotiating range is between the wanted "all rights" and the needed annual report and collateral rights plus liberal permission to use of the executive portraits.

My usual fee for "all rights" is beyond the client's budget, but I am not inclined to accept half my normal rate for any "all-rights" deal. Now I consider my negotiating range. I will grant "all rights" to all images for $20,000 or annual report rights only for $10,000, which is my bottom line. I have set up a $10,000 spread in those two menu options. My bottom line is the same dollar number that the prospect has indicated a willingness to pay. Understand that I know from experience that a prospect is usually willing to pay more than they initially indicate. Stating a lower number is the prospect's way of having room to move up.

I have set up a very wide range. Now I make the strategic decision and set a goal to sell all rights exclusively to the client for a period of two years (then the rights will revert back to me), and to give a perpetual exclusive rights license for use of the executive portraits for a fee of $15,000. That package meets their all their needs and an important want, namely, to have control over executives portraits.

When I present my offer to the client, I put all three options on the table. In doing so, I have rejected the client's offer of $10,000 for all rights and priced it well above the client's target. I have also created options. The $10,000 option meets their needs. The $20,000 option meets their wants. The $15,000 option fall between the two meeting a want and all needs. I have avoided rejecting the client's offer out of hand by making a subtle refusal through a higher fee for the all-rights demand. From here on it is tactical bargaining. My strategy has gone from the planning to the operational stage. Now I must engage in a negotiation.

I have also taken control of the direction of the discussion, and now I must make my middle option appear fair and reasonable to the client. Why shouldn't it be? It moves beyond meeting needs but does not reach for the dead end of trying to settle wants.

You might think, How can I get away with my strategy? Simple. When a prospect is going to spend $10,000 or more for a job, that prospect is counting on the photographer to deliver. The photography is a small part of the overall cost of producing the annual report. The prospect is not going to risk jeopardizing an expensive project by hiring the lowest bidder. The power I have is that I was deemed to be a photographer of the caliber that will make them feel secure. They will compromise to have that security.

This example shows why you have to understand the business you are in and the real priorities of your prospects. That is the underpinning of all negotiating strategy.

Rebuttals

Over time, as you gain experience negotiating, you will develop spontaneous rebuttals to some clients' routine claims. I have developed a few over the years. Here are some of them in script form.

Prospect: *I can hire a dozen other professionals to do the job for my price.*

Me: *No doubt you can. I can get you a person who will do it for half of your price, but ask yourself this question: Why are they willing to work for half the going rate? Could it be that they have a hard time getting work because they are not as good as those who charge fees like mine? Maybe it is because they have no credible experience. Maybe it is because they don't really understand what* *has to go into a job like yours. Maybe you ought to check with some of their past clients before you hire them. If you check with any of the contacts on the list I gave you, they will tell you why I am worth the fees I charge. I think the important question is do you want cheaper or better, not whether you can find a vendor who is cheaper. That's a given.*

Prospect: *I can't move on my fee offer. Our client is holding us to the budget and there is no room for an increase.*

Me: *Maybe you can cut back on something that won't make a difference. Cheaper work could easily mean inferior work and make a large and negative difference in the outcome. My work is the centerpiece of the project. Jeopardize it and the entire project is in jeopardy.*

Client: *Give me a break on this job, and I'll take care of you on the next one.*

Me: *I would consider that if I knew when and what the next one was going to be, and we set up the deal now, so I could get two purchase orders tomorrow.*

Client: *Why should I pay more for your work?*

Me: *For the reason you asked me to quote. You know I will get the job done when you need it and how you want it.*

Client: *We set up a budget for the work and your price exceeds it.*

Me: *I know it's hard to budget for work without knowing all the details the professional will consider when estimating it, but it seems that you miscalculated. You just can't expect that any professional can meet your expectations when you have not estimated the costs high enough. If you estimated the price to buy a BMW to be $45,000, and the dealer said there could be no possible sale of that model for less than $50,000, do you think the dealer* *would lower his price to meet your estimate shortfall? Your company wouldn't do that for its clients, and I cannot do it for mine.*

A SAMPLE DIALOG

To portray how an actual negotiation might unfold in my business, I have created a dialogue between a buyer (Pat) and a photographer (Happy). The dialogue begins after the photographer has offered his estimate with three options to the client. That estimate was sent a day or two before this conversation. It contained three options fashioned like that example given previously.

Happy: *Hello Pat. I wanted to check in to see if you have any questions about my estimate for the Slippery Snowmobile assignment. If you don't, I am ready to get started on the job.*

Pat: *I did look at it, and I have a few concerns that I do not have about the other two estimates I have for the job.*

Happy: *Let me resolve your concerns. What are they?*

Pat: *The option for different fees and rights are not what I expected. The other photographers just quoted the "all rights" that I asked for. When I compared their prices to yours for that deal, your fee was the highest.*

Happy: *I'm not surprised that my fee is high because my work is so well suited to your needs. I believe that is what got us together in the first place. I do my homework very carefully when I look for a client. I took the time to examine the fit between you and me before I even pro-*

moted myself to you. I was sure that you would see that I was particularly suited to do the Slippery Snowmobile work. It's that "particularly suited" that makes me cost a bit more than my competitors on this one. Getting those action shots you need out in the cold snowbanks of Colorado requires skill and experience like mine. I don't know how the other bidders are on this job, but I'm certain that I can do this job better than they can, and now I have to convince you of that....

Pat: *(interrupting) The fact still remains that you are higher priced. How can I justify that to the account executive and our client?*

Happy: *Ask them if they have Ford mechanics tune up their BMWs. Just kidding. I wouldn't try to justify it. Instead, I'd suggest that you suggest that my second option presents your client with a near-perfect deal. They get all the rights they really need, and they don't pay for something they want but don't need. Look, they get two years of exclusive, unlimited use, and they don't pay for a lifetime of use that won't be needed because of model changes. New models of the vehicles means new photos will be needed.*

Pat: *The continuing use is not the issue. The client does not want the images ever being used by another party. They have a fear that someday they will see one of their snowmobiles in a magazine story titled something like "Snowmobiles—Cripplers or Killers." They just want to be sure that something awful doesn't happen.*

Happy: *Very understandable. I can solve that problem one of two ways. I can agree in writing to never license the photographs to anyone for any reason. Or, I can give them all rights, if they agree to pay for any additional years of usage beyond the initial two years. How's that sound?*

Pat: *I think that they might buy the "all rights" with a guarantee of additional payment for extended usage. But the*

> price for your option two is still too high compared to the other photographers. So you have to come down.

Happy: I just effectively went from $20,000 to $15,000 and a promise. I think $15,000 is a very fair price for guaranteeing that your images will never get into the wrong hands and still giving you two years of unlimited and exclusive usage.

Pat: Yes, but our client has always bought all rights in perpetuity. I am guessing that they might compromise. I can't guarantee it.

Happy: Well, I am willing to sell all rights but not for the $10,000 you offered. I want double that amount to compensate for the fact that I will effectively never be able to get additional licensing fees if they decide to keep using the photos beyond two years. Look, you want to pay $10,000 and I want to double that for the deal you want. Level with me, and I might be able to come back with a better offer.

Pat: I've got a budget of $18,000 for the whole thing—fees, expenses, rights, etc. I can't even think about asking for more because the account executive is not about to jeopardize our relationship with Slippery when we can get an acceptable result from another photographer within that budget.

Happy: For $18,000 I can give you everything your client needs with the protection they think that they need. I am asking you, if I can structure the deal in a way that does what I just said, will I get the job?

At this point the negotiation can go in one of two directions. The buyer either acknowledges that he or she wants to work with Happy, or indicates no preference for Happy over the other bidders. Let's look at each scenario.

Scenario 1

Pat: *If you can meet my client's wants for no more than $18,000 for everything, I can give you the job.*

Happy: *I can do it. I need a little time to come up with the right wording. I'll call you back soon.*

Scenario 2

Pat: *Look Happy, you are a good photographer, but I have to go with the lowest qualified bidder to keep peace with the boss.*

Happy: *So where do I have to come in to get the job?*

Pat: *The low bid is $12,000 dollars for the whole deal with fees and expenses.*

Happy: *I have to think about it. I'll call you back?*

Working the Scenarios

Now Happy has to get his mind in gear. He has the parameters for the "real" deal. The prospect's client wants the maximum and permanent flexibility of an all rights deal even though the product life is about two years. In both scenarios the budget constraint makes the upper price limit $18,000 even though there is a competitive $12,000 offer. If Pat were happy with that photographer why would he continue entertaining Happy's options? He wouldn't. Pat wants Happy to do the work. Happy has no real competition. The prospect has already offered him the job, if he keeps his price below the $18,000 limit.

Happy has to come up with an explanation why his $20,000 offer just dropped to $18,000. However, there is no way to do that since the specifics of the deal have not changed. Happy has to fashion a reason for being able to come down in price. Happy has only to decide how to present his new offer to the prospect. The price is now established. Happy just has to have a reason for coming down $2,000. What might be worth $2,000?

Happy comes up with this solution. The job is for a highly recognized manufacturer in the winter sports business. That fact means letting that market segment know he did their work has promotional value for him. He can't use the images for promotion unless he gets an exception to the all rights deal. He will offer to do the work with all rights for the $18,000 specified by Pat. However he will ask for an exemption from the all rights deal to the extent that he can use the photographs to promote his business through his website and printed promotional materials. That has real value for him, and Pat will know that to be true. Pat will be pleased because he can get the work he wants for the dollars he has. The advertiser is not going to care because the use of those images in the way Happy proposes to use them is not competitive and is not going to expose them to hostile use by a publication. In fact, it might even serve to promote their products to any winter sports enthusiasts who see the promotional uses.

CALLING BACK

The next step is a call to Pat to present the revised offer. Since it meets Pat's price needs, and really offers Pat's client all it needs, it should fly without a problem. If it doesn't, Happy will have to negotiate to finesse the deal to a conclusion. He will do that by continually reasserting that the deal meets the client's wants. If Pat tries to force a better deal, Happy will remind Pat of the commitment that an $18,000 deal would fly. Happy has not lowered his price. He has obtained the value of his original price in a fee plus an award of valuable rights. If he simply lowered his price, Happy would be telling Pat that his price comes down for the asking. In that case, Pat will be sure to ask over and over again. A good deal is one in which items of equal value are exchanged. The successful business person gets the maximum value obtainable for his or her work in every deal made.

THE FINALE

The negotiation will end in one of two ways: Either you reach an agreement or you fail to do so. When you have reached an agreement, you should look over the notes you have been making throughout the process and summarize the items agreed upon. You have been keeping notes, haven't you? All good negotiators keep notes so that they can write up an agreement or complete a written agreement that embodies that which was agreed upon by the parties. After you confirm the details in the concluding review with a prospect you write up a confirmation and send or deliver it. The last thing that you want is for anyone's short-term memory to cause a subsequent disagreement over the terms that you originally agreed to. Confirming the agreed deal is the final and a critical act of the negotiation. Be sure not to skip that important action.

If you failed to reach an agreement, express how sorry you are that things did not work out, and confirm that you hope to be given another opportunity to work for the client on a future assignment. Then send a letter saying the same thing so that the prospect believes you mean it, and that you really are ready to come back and try again. Some people take failed negotiations to mean that the other party wants nothing to do with them in the future. You should firmly dispel that thought if you want to build your clientele and bank account.

Be Thorough

There are no shortcuts in negotiating. You have to consider intangible fears like performance issues and value issues like time and fees. You will have to understand your prospect's positions and separate the wants from the needs, so you can develop a range of alternatives to build a compromise around. Never skip confirming your agreements unless you like to negotiate disputes (and if you do, maybe you ought to try law school). Always keep the door open when negotiations fail. Tomorrow might bring a better job with a better budget or relaxed demands. That is the one you have been looking for so don't miss the opportunity to get a shot at it. Thoroughness is a key component of negotiating—before the fact when doing homework, during the discussions, and after the fact when wrapping up.

Chapter Eight

NEGOTIATING PURCHASES

If you can negotiate from the seller's side, you can easily adapt to negotiating from the buyer's side. Even though you might not have evidence of it from the behavior of the buyers you have dealt with, the principles, psychology, and tactics are the same. A good buyer does homework, develops a plan, and then engages a seller in a negotiation. This chapter will focus on techniques that you can use to gain some advantage in negotiating your purchases.

NEGOTIATING OPPORTUNITIES

It takes at least two willing parties to have a negotiation, so that is the first criterion for a recognizing a negotiating opportunity. Not everything you purchase is open for negotiation. Your groceries, insurance, electric-service fees, and many other daily necessities are locked into established price lists that great numbers of consumers are subject to. Generally you will find a negotiating opportunity when you are buying items that you do not buy frequently or that you buy in volume when there is enough margin between seller's cost and offered price to leave room for a negotiation. In my business cameras and lenses are examples of small-ticket items. Buildings and automobiles are examples of large-ticket items.

SMALL EQUIPMENT PURCHASES

I don't want to create any false expectations about being able to negotiate for small-ticket items. Whether you will have an opportunity to do it depends on circumstances. Since I am in the photography business, I can offer photography equipment as a good example, because it is sold with a slim margin by high-volume dealers. However, the same strategy can apply to a host of purchases. There isn't much room to negotiate the price of a $1,000 camera if the dealer is only making $50 over cost on it and is selling twenty of them a day. This being said, opportunities to negotiate do exist and can be made. How do you recognize or create the opportunity?

I previously mentioned "margin." Like you, the seller has a bottom line. For the small business there is no benefit in taking a loss on the sale of equipment, but there is a benefit in making some money instead of none. So you have to ask yourself, What incentive will motivate a seller to lower a price? The answer is enough cash to make cash flow a bit easier, or a way to move an older product off the shelf to make room for newer ones.

Suppose you are a photographer, and you are going to change camera systems because technological advances have made your current gear obsolete. You might be purchasing a camera and back-up unit and a few lenses. Your regional camera dealer's prices are always higher than the mail-order houses from which you usually buy single items of equipment. The problem you encounter in doing so is that the shipping charges can eat up your savings, and sometimes the items get back ordered. The biggest headache is when a piece of equipment is faulty when it comes out of the original box. The mail-order houses have quick systems for taking your money, but they do not always keep pace when it comes to returning it or replacing defective merchandise. A local dealer will be better at that.

Additionally, you want to trade in your existing system to reduce the out-of-pocket payment for the new gear. The mail-order house will take trade-ins, but you have to ship the gear to them to be inspected so there will be a period that you will have no equipment handy, and the value of your trade-in will not be easily negotiable due to logistics and the fact that it is nearly obsolete. Finally, if you buy from the mail-order house, you will have to pay when you place the order, not when you receive the gear. If all or any part of it is back ordered, you are tying up cash without benefit. You will also have to insure the shipment at extra cost, because the risk of losing an expensive shipment in transport is not one you care to take. Buying locally is beginning to look better and better, if you can just get a competitive price.

STRATEGIC BUYING

When you are buying, always remember that the seller is in the same shoes you are in when you are trying to make a deal. He doesn't want to lose a sale that he can make money on, as long as the hidden costs are not high. By "hidden costs," I mean hours invested to make the sale, grief from the buyer, and maybe even having the word get out that special deals can be cut. So you want to have your ducks lined up in a row—that is, know exactly *what* you want to buy, and what is the best price you can get somewhere else.

You also want to have a deal in mind. Don't count on the seller being creative. A busy retailer has little opportunity to get creative at the individual sale level. Just as you would prepare a proposal for a buyer, prepare a proposal for the seller. Having the total price you have been quoted elsewhere is important. When the seller sees a list of camera gear on paper, it is just that. When he sees a large dollar number on paper, he has to pay attention. Wouldn't you? The total dollar figure will give the seller some idea of what the profit on the sale might be. Most likely he knows the difference between his usual price and that being charged by his mail-order competition. With a bit of quick math he can get a feel for what he will make from the sale.

You should know the total cost to you, if you were to buy it from the mail-order house or other highly competitive supplier. By "total cost" I mean insured and delivered to your doorstep. You also should prepare a list of the gear you wish to trade in, if any. If you do, you will be the seller and he will be the buyer for that trade-in part of the transaction.

Finally, approach the seller about a special deal in private, not over the counter in a customer-filled store; he doesn't want to give the impression to others that he actually discounts merchandise when approached. You might send him a note or email saying that you would like to purchase the equipment on the enclosed list. Mention that you will be happy to come in and show him your used gear and discuss the price of the new equipment.

The next thing you have to do is to think about what kind of options you can present. Chances are he is not going to spend a lot of time thinking about this. He has a bottom-line price, and it probably has little margin of profit. In other words, the sale may not be as important to him as you would like it to be. What can you do to increase its importance? The answer is to think strategically.

STRATEGIC THINKING

Think about your counterpart's position in business. What big problem does he encounter and how can you motivate him through your understanding? He faces the same problem that you face. He is continually dealing with maintaining adequate cash flow without tapping reserves or borrowing money. How can your sale help him?

PROPOSAL TIMING

Most merchants pay their bills to suppliers within ten to thirty days after the end of the month billed. It is the period when they need the most cash on hand. If you can provide an influx of cash during the the period near the end of a month, your sale is much more important than if you buy mid-month. You want to negotiate your deal when the seller is most in need of cash. That is a time when the percentage of profit is not as important as the cash itself. Time your negotiations for that period, and be ready to pay fast. Many dealers will make great deals to get cash when they need it.

Cash or Credit Card?

If you can pay cash you can make a better deal. The merchant has to pay a discount fee to the credit card company for every credit card sale. The percentage varies depending upon the seller's level of sales, but it is reasonable to assume that a seller loses three percent of the sale in the discount fee that the credit card company exacts. When you are give a price it usually has that three percent built in. When purchasing equipment, after I am quoted a price, I always say something to this effect. "If I pay you by credit card you will lose about three percent of that price to the credit card company. If I pay you by check what percentage will you take off the price? By the way, I am happy to wait until the check clears before taking possession because I know merchants worry about bad checks."

Avoid Snares and Add Incentive

You have your old gear to trade in. But that is not cash for the merchant until he sells it. Since a trade in would effectively decrease the amount of cash he would receive, it would decrease the motivation to make a better deal at bill-paying time. You can add incentive to the deal by asking him to sell your old equipment on consignment. That way, he has no cash outlay or reduction for adding it to inventory, and you actually get more money on consignment than through a trade-in. On a trade you will get about one-half of the used selling price. When you sell on consignment, you can pay the dealer as little as 25 percent of the sale, and your gain is greater, albeit with a longer wait for the money than with a trade-in. You do recall that in an earlier part of this book I mentioned that having money makes it easier to negotiate good deals.

Some dealers won't deal in consignments or purchase used gear that is obsolete or approaching obsolete. Most customers want new technology, not old. Making your old equipment part of a purchase of new gear can be a snare in which you get caught. (The good negotiator sometimes sets traps into which he himself might step.) You can always sell the gear on an Internet auction or donate it to a charity for a tax deduction.

PITCHING THE DEAL

The pitch is simple. You want to buy locally, but you can't overspend to do so. You need the best price that you can get, and it has to be equal to that of the mail-order house. To get that deal, you are prepared to make the deal right now and pay right now.

This is a simple negotiating strategy. Equipment that the dealer has already paid for and has on the shelves is like having money sitting on your shelves that you cannot spend. When a dealer needs money for cash flow, selling off inventory is a great way to get it. You are just facilitating the process with strategic timing.

RESEARCH THE TIMING

Purchasing large-ticket items offers the best opportunity for negotiating, because these items usually have the kind of margin built into their prices that gives the seller some leeway. An automobile ßis a perfect example. If you have ever purchased a car, you know just what I mean: The dealer probably started out offering you a price that is lower than the sticker price. How much lower you got the price is dependent upon your negotiating expertise.

Researching buying cycles and timing your purchase during a slower buying cycle will help you negotiate a better deal. A furnace with installation will cost less in the spring than in the winter. You can research buying cycles on the Internet.

Let's continue with the example of the car purchase. As a strategically thinking negotiator, you will take the time to learn about car-buying cycles. You will learn that most cars are sold in the spring or fall. The spring is the beginning of mild weather and precedes the summer driving season. Many people want a new car before summer vacation or for the springtime, when they make many day outings. They also don't like their cars to face the abuses of winter when brand spanking new. Many others buy cars in the fall, because the new models are coming out, and dealers offer special prices on current models to get rid of inventory. What does this tell you? It tells you that the car dealers have lots of business in the spring and fall, so those are not strategically advantageous times to buy a car.

When you research car-buying trends, you find out that the worst sales period for car dealers is late December through early January. The holiday season keeps many people engaged in other buying, the weather is usually not good, taxes start to be on people's minds, and, for some, seasonal depression is at its peak. That makes it a perfect time to buy a car. No one else is, and the dealership has bills to pay.

The best time to buy is between December 24 and January 5. Hardly any cars sell during that period. You even have the added advantage of buying a previous year's left-over, which will drop in price on January 1 because it is last year's model. Yes, timing is important, and as the buyer, you can set the time you are ready to buy the car.

If that end of year timing does not work for you, then try for the end of a month. Dealers that meet monthly sales quotas set by the manufacturer earn dealer incentives. Those incentives boil down to money. As the end of the month approaches, some dealers who have not yet met the sales quota will offer deep discounts to make the sale, because the dealer incentive is more valuable than a small profit or even a small loss on a car. Remember, timing is often an important factor in negotiating.

COMPETITIVE PRESSURE

You understand how competitive pressure is used against a seller, because it happens to you all the time. Now you get to turn the tables. Certainly you understand that you will need to comparison shop to get prices on the car you want from different dealers. That applies some competitive pressure. But how much does it apply?

If you want an X-ray 500 sedan, and you get three prices from three different dealers, you have reinforced in all their minds that you want an X-ray 500. I said want. Sellers want you to want what they are selling. It makes their job easier, and they don't feel as much pressure as they would if you were also considering a competitor's car. A competitive dealer selling X-ray 500s is not as threatening as a dealer selling a comparative car made by a different manufacturer. X-ray 500 dealers know the dealer's actual price and manufacturer's dealer incentives, since they apply to all X-ray dealers. They know successful competitive X-ray dealers will stop lowering price at a certain point, because they have been competing with them for years. They know their competition.

You should introduce some unusual competition into the mix. While you do not want to do it at the outset, eventually you will let the X-ray dealers know that you are also considering and pricing Y-Streak 300, a competitive manufacturer's model meant to compete with the X-ray 500. By doing so, you will be saying that you want an X-ray 500, but you don't need it, because a Y-Streak 300 will do just fine. You will put a chink in the X-ray dealer's psychological mind-set. Just time that tactic right, and I'll explain the best timing shortly.

The X-ray dealer can only guess at what incentives the manufacturers are offering Y-Streak dealers to move cars. These are not buyer incentives like rebates and low interest. These are special deals and terms for dealers. Now he has competition that he doesn't fully understand. That's real competition.

To get more advantage, don't mention the Y-Streak competition until after you have gotten the best price you can by forcing some competition among the X-ray dealers. Get price quotes from three X-ray 500 dealers. Dealers are not going to give you a firm price unless you are committed to buying from them. At least that is what they lead you to believe. Don't buy that! You are the prospective buyer and you have to let them know you are not the average buyer who can be led down a path the dealer likes. Insist on a firm price or threaten to walk out saying that you have firm prices from other dealers and you expect one from them if they want a chance at a sale.

Once you have the best price from an X-ray 500 dealer, force that dealer to compete with the Y-Streak dealer. You will quickly find that there is still margin for the dealer to give up. The dealer has beaten his usual competition. Now make him beat the competition he fears the most – the other manufacturer's dealer.

You can easily make a trade-off when buying a product that has upgrades, like the feature packages on a car. Price a lower-feature package than you want. When you have the dealer competing against the other manufacturer's dealer, and you have pushed the price to its rock bottom, imply that you are going to take the competitor's deal. Then offer a trade-off. You will take his deal, if he will upgrade your car to have the package you want for dealer's invoice cost. You may not get the dealer's price, but you will get a big discount, because the feature packages have a greater percentage of profit than the base car and basic packages. Frills are wants, and wants cost more. Buy yours cheaper.

BARTERING

Exchanging goods and services for other goods and services offers ample opportunity to negotiate especially when the trade is for services. Goods usually have a discoverable market value. You can easily find the price of fifty bags of cement and if you happen to be trading golf clubs for the cement the value of the clubs is also discoverable. The trick in negotiating bartering for goods is to know the value of each item in the trade. If the fifty bags of cement cost $300 and the set of golf clubs cost $500, you will want $200 in cash in addition to the bags of cement, or you will want more bags of cement or something else of value to make it a fair trade.

Bartering services is more difficult that bartering goods. The value of services is not always discoverable. Of course if an accountant with an established rate of $200 per hour is bartering for legal services from a lawyer with an established rate of $400, the $200 difference is clear. However, most real bartering opportunities for services are between individuals who are unlikely to have a single established rate.

Recently, I was approached by a small contractor to design, write, and provide photographs for a new website. I do not have an hourly rate for that kind of work. Instead, I price by the project. Coincidently, I needed some repairs to the deck in my yard. Some boards needed to be replaced, and after that was done, the deck would have to be power-washed and sealed. I asked the contractor if he was interested in bartering. He was. Now we faced the problem of determining a fair trade of services; that meant we would likely get caught up in a disagreement over whose time was more valuable. He asked me what I would charge for the website project. I priced it at $1,600 for a basic, five-page website. He then told me that his price for the work on the deck would be $2,000. The $400 difference did not work for me. I told him so and mentioned that I could certainly shop around and get a better price than his, so we had to find a way to make a more even swap. Here is what I suggested: We would both write down the number of hours we would have to work to complete our respective projects. Then we would see how similar the time we would work was. He agreed, and we both wrote a number on a paper and swapped papers. My time quote was two days. His was two and a half days. We had a gap to close.

I have power-washed and sealed my deck in the past. It took about four hours to wash it and about the same to seal it. Certainly it would not take him any longer. I made an offer. It went like this: I know the washing and sealing is a day of work, and I estimated that the repairs would take maybe four to six hours. His total time commitment would be about the same as mine, two days. I told him that I understood he thought it would take two and a half hours, but that I was not prepared to pay for that extra half day. I suggested an even trade, pushing the idea that I would buy the materials for the deck project, so all he had was an outlay of time.

I clinched the deal with another thought for him. I could do what he wanted, and I wanted to barter. Any other person he contacted to do the website was unlikely to barter, wanting cash instead. His choice was get his website done with no cash outlay or pay for the work. He made the even swap. Why? Because the cash-saving was more important to him than a few extra hours that he might have to spend on the job. I call that presenting a vanishing opportunity. Cash talks when you spend it or when you save it.

Remember the Basics

The examples in this chapter demonstrate the benefit of doing research into the nature of the seller's business when you are going to purchase a high-priced item—that is, when you are actually likely to have an opportunity to negotiate. The methods and considerations portrayed here can be applied to other products and services. The critical similarity is, no matter what is to be purchased, that doing research, understanding the seller's hidden needs, and applying real competitive pressure will help you negotiate the best price you can get.

Chapter Nine

CONFLICT RESOLUTION

In every business person's life there comes a time when you will be confronted with a hostile disagreement, that is, a serious conflict. It might be over the terms of an agreement that you are being accused of breaching. It could be a dispute over the quality of services performed or the quality of goods sold. Regardless of what the dispute is, conflict resolution through negotiation is likely the best way out. The alternative is legal action, and that means big bucks, a lot of your time, and an emotion-draining process.

Conflict resolution is a negotiating specialty, and many books have been written about the topic. While I am not an expert in that field, I have on many occasions been called upon to negotiate a resolution to a serious conflict. I gained a lot of experience in this area by serving as the executive director of American Society of Media Photographers for fifteen years. I was called upon to represent photographers in industry discussions when publishers and photographers were not seeing eye to eye. During that time, I learned that traditional negotiating tactics worked in resolving conflicts. I also learned that there was an added dimension to conflict negotiations that was not part of sales negotiations. I'll elaborate.

RESOLVABLE OR NOT

The first question you have to ask when considering resolving a conflict is what exactly is the conflict: Is it fact (position-based) or intangible (policy-based)? Facts and interpretations of facts can be worked through to agreement more readily than differences in principle or policy. Many conflicts have both. When that happens, you deal *first* with the positions (the opposite of sales negotiation), because you could simply iron out a deal that makes the principle a non-issue. Once you identify the issues in conflict, you have to decide whether they can be resolved by mutual agreement. If a demand is unreasonable and neither party is willing to compromise, then you are unlikely to reach a resolution.

The next thing you must assess is what the cost of failing to resolve the conflict will be. Will you lose a supplier or client? Will there be no consequences? Can you or the other party afford the consequences? That assessment will govern how much energy you apply and how much risk you can take.

COOL AND OBJECTIVE

When someone tells you did something wrong, it can result in a defensive reaction because you may take it personally. The person making the claim is trying to protect his interest, not damage yours; you would do the same thing if you thought your interests were being compromised. People can disagree without being disagreeable. Maintaining a professional demeanor and objectivity will ensure that cooler heads prevail. This is a key factor in resolving a disagreement. If your counterpart is acting unprofessional, politely point out that his demeanor is impeding the resolution attempt. If the behavior does not improve, consider calling off the process until the person is ready to approach a resolution attempt in a professional manner.

AVOID THE STRAW MAN

A "straw man" is a sham argument meant to be defeated. It is like a red herring in negotiating, that is, not a real issue but something brought in to influence outcomes. Separate the real issue from the straw man issue, because the only purpose of a straw man issue is to pile on and put a person on the defensive. This goes back to the importance of being objective discussed above.

SPEAK CAREFULLY

You cannot unsay something. Once it is out there it is not coming back. If you say something that is hurtful or disrespectful you can make a person angry, and that can lead to a breakdown of the resolution process. You should also speak with a calm, low voice, as that is perceived as conciliatory and will help keep your counterpart calm.

FORGET THE PAST

If you have had disagreements with the other party in the past, do not bring them up or allow them to be brought up for discussion. It is counterproductive to relive past disagreements. Stay focused on the issue(s) at hand.

UNDERSTAND VULNERABILITIES

Everyone has something to lose. When resolving a conflict, the other party's vulnerabilities are your leverage. Everyone has vulnerabilities. I can best portray how vulnerabilities come into play through a real-life example.

As ASMP's executive director I was called upon to represent the interests of photographers who had made the images that were used in a special edition of a popular weekly sports magazine. The publisher published a 35th anniversary issue of the magazine, and the content was made up of small reproductions of all of the covers of the magazine up to that time. There were 1,600 covers reproduced.

Photographers who shot for that magazine over the decades worked under an agreement with the publisher that basically said they would be paid for any additional use of their images after the first publication unless the use were promotional rather than editorial. When the anniversary issue was published, photographers were caught by surprise. Many called the magazine to inquire about payment, and they were told there would be none. My phone rang all day long for several days. Photographers were asking for action. My next step was to set up a meeting with the managing editor of the magazine. He advised that he would have the magazine's attorney on hand for the meeting. I advised that I would bring ASMP's attorney.

During the meeting the publisher took a simple position. Knowing that it did not have to pay for promotional uses, it said that the anniversary issue was nothing more than a huge promotion to generate subscriptions. Remember how I urged you get the facts before you negotiate? Well, I had anticipated that argument. I got in touch with several of the affected photographers who subscribed to the magazine to get their copies. I discovered that the issue—like all other issues of the magazine—had been mailed as second-class mail. The price for mailing a magazine second class was based upon the number of magazines and the ratio of advertising to editorial pages. The more editorial pages, the lower the price. Armed with that knowledge, I asked the publisher for a copy of the second-class mail application for the anniversary issue. They produced it. It declared the issue to be 40 percent ads and 60 percent editorial. So that meant the reproduced covers were *not* promotional, as the publisher had stated.

At this point, the publisher had lost Round One and was on the defensive, which is where a misrepresentation will usually get you. To recover, the publisher took a new tack. Relying on its lawyer, it declared that the magazine had the right to use the work because a provision in the copyright law superseded the agreement they had relied upon for years. This sent the lawyers into days of arguing without a resolution. I decided that enough was enough. I had had our lawyers draw up a complaint for filing a lawsuit in the names of some of the photographers involved. I put it on the table thinking that the publisher might be inclined to settle rather than fight a court battle. I was so wrong!

The publisher responded to my threat of a lawsuit by saying that it could (and it *really* could) drag out a suit and make it prohibitively expensive for ASMP to fight. I began to calculate. I had to recover, because my bluff had not worked. And then lightning struck, and I had the answer. I told the publisher that I knew that it could and would outspend ASMP in any court case, but I added a twist. I told them that I would set up a special legal defense fund and ask photographers to (these are my actual words) "Stop the rape of photographers by the —— magazine by supporting the ASMP legal action." I went on to say: "Photographers do not give a rat's about your ridiculous position. You agreed to pay them, and now you refuse. Let's go to court. You will likely win the case. You will lose the war. When all is said and done you will be seen as a publisher that cannot be trusted. Photographers will not work for you." I then gave them seven days to agree to pay or ASMP would file the suit. I walked out.

A few days later, I was in a hotel room in Kansas City. The phone rang. It was the publisher's chief legal counsel. He said that, in the spirit of fairness, the publisher would pay the photographers. I told him that "fairness" worked for me. The photographers were paid. Better yet, a year later, when the same publisher wanted to do a cover issue for a different magazine, it called me in to discuss how to handle payments to the photographers. I obliged.

The resolution of the matter was based upon what the publisher had to lose. ASMP risked losing the legal case, but even if that happened, ASMP would have fared well in the minds of photographers because it had tried to protect their rights. On the other hand, the publisher was in a lose-lose situation. If it got into a dragged-out legal case with photographers, it would be reported in the trade press every time there was a development. That would be bad PR. If it won the case, the publisher would come off as having beaten up on its suppliers. If it lost the case, all would be for naught, and the publisher would just look bad for not paying up without being sued. Those pitfalls would make photographers of the caliber the publisher needed wary about working for the publisher, which relied upon high-quality sports photography. This is a classic example of how the cost of failing to resolve a conflict can have a price too high to pay.

FINDING A HIDDEN LEVER

Conflicts normally are about oral or written agreements broken in whole or in part. Written agreements are better than oral agreements because the terms are in black and white and not simply a matter of recollection as in the case of oral agreements. Understanding the agreements one is party to is very important. That is why this book has one chapter devoted entirely to negotiating contracts. Every deal you make is a contract. There is an offer, acceptance, and consideration changes hands. So understanding the responsibilities of parties to a contract is important when a conflict develops. Here is another example of a conflict resolution.

A friend had just renewed an apartment lease for a one-year term. There were ninety days to go on the original lease at the time of renewal. During that ninety-day period, the lessee received a job offer that required that he relocate. Taking the job, he informed the landlord that he could not honor the new lease because he had to move to another city. The landlord was not receptive to the news, and he demanded that the lessee pay three months' rent for termination of the new lease, even though it had not even come into force yet. The lease called for three months' rent to make an early termination. The lessee took the position that because the new lease would not come into effect for another forty-five days, he could cancel it at will, as the landlord had adequate time to rent the unit to another person. The landlord rejected that argument out of hand and demanded the three months' rent again. The lessee refused. The parties went back and forth for a month only to find themselves in stalemate. Finally, the landlord threatened to take the matter to small claims court.

My friend asked me if I had any ideas about how to resolve the matter without going to court. I did. I suggested that he send the landlord a letter demanding that the landlord inform him of three things: Where the apartment's availability had been advertised, how often it had been advertised, and how many people seeking apartments had been shown the unit in question. The answers to those questions would serve as leverage in resolving the conflict.

When a contract is breached, it is the duty of the parties to mitigate the damages caused by the breach. In the case of the apartment, the only way the landlord could mitigate the damages would be to try to rent the apartment. When the landlord refused to answer those questions, I suggested to my friend that he tell the landlord to file the small court claim, and that he, the lessee, would demand that information in court. He was entitled to such information in a legal action. My friend followed my advice. The landlord came back with a settlement offer. He would keep the security deposit, equal to one month's rent, and drop the demand for payment of three months' rent. My friend accepted. Conflict resolved.

The hidden leverage was a performance issue. I knew from reading local publications that the landlord never advertised available apartments. It was a popular building and people were drawn to it. I knew that the landlord had not shown the apartment to anyone because he would have had to notify the lessee in advance of entering the apartment to show it. Since the landlord had failed to even attempt to mitigate damages, he would be vulnerable in any legal action. My suggestion increased the landlord's risk factor and reduced the likelihood of his receiving an award of damages in the amount claimed. He decided the try to keep the money he had already received from the lessee rather than try to get more. So it ended up costing my friend $1,200 instead of $3,600. The hidden leverage was ramping up the risk factor.

WITS BEFORE WORDS

The two previous examples show just how important it is to do one's homework. The good conflict negotiator always digs deep for any information it can find related to the dispute. That information is then evaluated to see what applies.

The risk factor often plays into settlements of conflicts. What a party has to lose is important, and it is important that you understand what that loss might be for your counterpart. Then weaving that into the discussion at the right time is critical. I believe that increasing the risk is best done late in a conflict negotiation, because it will increase hostility. Hostility is generally counterproductive in a negotiation. You should only allow it or create it when it becomes clear that a resolution will not be reached without it.

Negotiation is a game of wits before it is an exercise of words.

Chapter Ten

LEARNING WHAT THIS BOOK TEACHES

In the Babylonian Talmud it says: "Learning is more important that practice because learning leads to practice." Like most ancient wisdom, there is an undeniable truth in those words. Practice is a way to polish what we know. Learning is getting to know what we will later practice.

FIRST THINGS FIRST

Learning to negotiate starts with having a solid knowledge of the topic. The first five chapters of this book are: 1) The Nature of Negotiation, 2) Traits of a Good Negotiator, 3) Planning for a Negotiation, 4) Psychological Aspects of Negotiating, and 5) Negotiating Strategy and Tactics. These five chapters lay the groundwork for the rest of the book's content. They are the most important chapters in the book, because they address the groundwork on which all negotiating efforts are built.

At this point in the book, you are nearly done. You might be anxious to apply what you have learned. You should do that. You should also read the first five chapters again, and maybe even several times over. The mind-set of a negotiator is fortified by understanding the basics, just like the mind-set of a photographer is when it comes to doing photography. You didn't learn the basics of photography by a casual reading on the topic. You studied the topic. And you learned the topic. There is no reason to think that learning to negotiate is any different from learning to photograph.

TAKE NOTES

Learning requires discipline. One discipline is note taking. You can kill two birds with one stone by taking notes as you read. First, it will provide you with a means to refresh your memory periodically, and, second, it will help you practice the process of note taking, which is an indispensable skill for the negotiator. If you keep your notes neat and concise, they can be used as a reference in real-life negotiations. Trying to quickly refresh your mind by skimming a book is much harder than reviewing a set of concise notes.

HOMEWORK SHEETS

You can also make lists of questions to which you want the answers for planning your negotiations. Who, what, when, where, how, and why are important interrogatories. When you reread Chapter 3, you should make lists of questions based upon the examples given in the chapter. I purposely did not include a list of questions for you in this book, because I know that you will learn the questions, rather than just use the ones could give you, if you make the lists yourself. And you want to learn, not just use.

REFLECT ON YOURSELF

As you re-read about the nature of a negotiator, reflect on your own nature. Do you have the traits of a successful negotiator? Do you have to adapt? If you have to adapt, just what traits do you have to work on and how can you do this? The answer is to develop a sense of self-awareness, and to discipline yourself where you are lacking. If you know yourself to be a poor listener, ask yourself if you are listening when someone is talking to you. If you are not, concentrate on what they are saying. The success of a negotiator is connected to the ability to understand another's point of view. You cannot do that unless you listen to them. If a negotiator acts like the world revolves around him, it will be a very small world doing the circling.

Consider each trait of a good negotiator, assess your level of achievement in that area, and then work on those areas in which you are lacking. It is a matter of mental discipline. You have to exercise mental discipline to be a good negotiator, so you might as well start doing so in a self-assessment process.

CONTINUOUS LEARNING

As a business person you must continually learn about your business. There is always some new insight to be gained. Read about it, attend seminars and workshops, and look for expert-led discussions on the Internet. Being a good negotiator requires continual learning. There are dozens, if not hundreds, of books on the topic. There are seminars on the topic. You should read other books and participate in seminars. Most books and seminars are general in nature. Unlike this book, they are not written for a specific audience. But that does not matter. After reading this book, which has been geared to the small business owner, other books will make more sense to you. You will easily adapt the information to your own specialized need. The same thing is true of seminars.

LEARN THROUGH REVIEW

As you engage in negotiating, you will undoubtedly find yourself in situations when you are stumped for an answer or a tactic to employ. While most of us like to forget such uncomfortable moments (for our own peace of mind), I assure you that your peace of mind will be much greater when you purposefully remember what went wrong. By reviewing such moments you can reconsider what you might have said to a statement or question that you were not prepared for. You will eventually hear the same statement or question again in the future. If you have reviewed and reconsidered the matter, you will be ready to deal with it next time. Each time you have a bad moment while negotiating, review the moment in your mind. Consult this book or your notes and ask what did you do wrong, what tactic could you have employed, what answer might you have given. In doing so, you will develop an arsenal for future negotiations.

LEARN THROUGH PRACTICE

Practice in itself is not learning. It is developing skill based upon how you use what you have learned. Practice offers you the opportunity to learn because of it. By practicing negotiating, you will find your weaknesses before you engage in the real thing. Practice with a colleague who also wants to perfect negotiating skills. Switch roles as buyer and seller. Develop scenarios that mimic real-life experiences in business.

Review your practice sessions just as you would review a real negotiating session. Look for your weak points during the practice, and consider what you might have done differently. Then try running through the same scenario again. It is just like training as an athlete or performer. You practice each play, step, and action. When you make a mistake, you review what it was. Then you do it again until you get it right. Each practice helps you learn more about what you are doing.

TALK TO YOURSELF

Don't worry about being seen as crazy. Talk to yourself as if you were in a negotiation. Years ago, I met a champion chess player. I asked how he learned to play chess. He said that his father had taught him the basics. He learned from experience of actual games. He learned through practice by playing with others. But he also learned by playing against himself. He would play both sides, in effect trying to stump himself. He would set up a terrible chess scenario on the board and than play to fight through that scenario.

You can do a similar thing. Ask yourself that question or present to yourself that demand that you fear the most. Then build your answer to it. Speak your reply to yourself. You will know when you have it right. Of course, close the door to the room, or people will think you are nuts.

ACKNOWLEDGE THE ESSENTIALS

You have to develop a feeling for the quintessence of negotiating, not just a knowledge of the methods. The heart of the process is based upon the sound principles stated in this book. They are not my personal concoctions. They are time-proven and well-recognized principles of negotiating. Some of the most important of these principles are restated below in the words of men who considered the topic of negotiating long before I did.

- The Fair Deal:
  "The old idea of a good bargain was a trans-action in which one man got the better of another. The new idea of a good contract is a transaction which is good for both parties."
  > Louis Brandeis, 1856-1941
  > U. S. Supreme Court Justice
  > Business—A Profession

- Two Willing Parties:
  "A man whose word will not inform you at all what he means or will do is not a man you can bargain with. You must get out of that man's way, or put him out of yours."

Thomas Carlyle, 1795-1881
Scottish Essayist
On Heroes and Hero Worship

- Options Are Essential:
  "The greatest strength of the negotiator lies in thinking up new proposals as soon as strong objections are made."
  > Walther Rathenau, 1867-1922
  > CEO, AEG (General Electric Germany)
  > Reflexionen, 1908

- Exercise Patience:
  "Don't negotiate with yourself. Have the patience to wait for the other fellow to make a counter-offer after you have made one."
  > Richard Smith
  > Partner, Smith, McWorter & Pachter
  > Speech, Washington D.C. 2/12/1988

MAKE THE EFFORT

Your success as negotiator will depend on how well you have learned to negotiate. That will depend on how much study and practice you have done. It will also depend upon how well you perfect your knowledge and skills by the review and revision of attempts gone awry. Success is always about the effort of applying knowledge. Learning not only provides the knowledge, but it also motivates additional effort. Make the effort to learn how to negotiate. As you learn, you will feel like making additional effort. Remember: Success feeds on success. Make the effort now, and you will be successful in your negotiations. That can lead to a very successful business.

GLOSSARY

A

Abstract issues: Issues associated with principle bargaining, such as business policies.

Accommodate: To compromise on certain points so that a deal can be made, rather than staunchly insisting that the other party yield to one's demands.

Advantages: Aspects providing leverage over a business partner or rival that can help one side strike a better deal for itself in negotiations. One side having an advantage over the other makes a fair deal unlikely.

Aggressive buyer: Like a hard negotiator, an aggressive buyer is usually very direct, makes no attempt to befriend the other party, makes difficult demands, displays a resistance to compromise, speaks loudly, uses intimidation tactics, and seems unapproachable.

Alternative-development: Part of the negotiation planning process by which one side carefully prepares a B list of contingencies in the event that the other party rejects their A list requests.

Authority: The power to make decisions, give permission, approve requests, and manage and oversee subordinates' actions. In a negotiation, one either has or does not have the authority to approve or make a deal with another party. One can claim a lack of authority in order to force the other party's position downward. See also *limited authority*.

B

Bankrolled: A circumstance where an individual or group has sufficient funds or is being provided funds for some purpose (to make a deal, to cover living/business expenses, etc).

Bargaining: Similar to haggling, bargaining is the part of the negotiation process when two sides discuss terms, conditions, and prices until they are mutually agreeable. See also *principle bargaining* and *positional bargaining*.

Bargaining range: The wiggle room a party has at any point in a negotiation. Within these parameters a deal may be considered agreeable.

Bartering: Exchanging goods and services for other goods and services.

Bold response: When a business prospect makes an unreasonable demand and the other party calls their bluff, knowing that their own refusal to bend to the other party's demands could damage their business relationship.

Bottom-line: The amount of profit that is realized after all expenses and taxes have been paid the minimum amount necessary to maintain a healthy business; the deciding or crucial factor. See also *bottom-line fee*.

"Bread and butter" jobs: Averagely lucrative jobs that help a business meet its bottom line.

Broken record: A technique in which one party repeatedly asks for something until they get it.

Businesslike: Professional—does not exclude being friendly; efficient, practical, realistic.

Business strategy: A chosen method or course of conducting business with someone designed to make one's own business more successful. The most important aspects are sales and finances.

Buying cycles: The trend where a commodity is bought frequently during one period of time (and will thus be more expensive) and that same commodity is rarely purchased during another period (and will therefore be less expensive). Example: air conditioner installation.

C

Candor: The state or quality of being open, frank, and free from bias. Showing candor can be an excellent way to bring a negotiating discussion that has been going in circles to a conclusion.

"Champagne" jobs: Jobs that provide a significant boost in financial and psychic power.

Client company: The company that will pay you in a deal or for a good or service you provide.

Communications director: The person who performs PR and HR duties for a company.

Compensation: Something (usually a financial reward) exchanged for goods or services.

Competitive interests: The bargaining points of the negotiation, including things like price, deadlines, terms, and conditions.

Competitive power: Having knowledge and a position as a buyer to put pressure on and discourage a seller from doing any more than meeting their absolute financial needs when pricing a good or service.

Competitive pressure: Pressure applied to a seller when the buyer forces them to lower the cost of their good or service or risk losing a sale.

Competitor: A business that provides the same goods or services as one's own business. Competitors share the same pool of customers.

Complex negotiation: Negotiations that include multiple factors like deadlines, deposits, expense reimbursements, insurance requirements, etc.

Complementary interests: Issues that do not have to be resolved because the parties agree on them at the outset of the negotiation.

Compromise: A settlement of differences by mutual concessions. An essential tool of negotiation.

Concession: Acceptance of the other party's demands or negotiating limits for the sake of moving a negotiation forward. A valuable and necessary part of negotiations, concessions demonstrate good faith and a company's willingness to cooperate with the other side.

Concrete issues: In positional bargaining, concrete issues include physical and/or accurately measurable things like money, materials, and time. Concrete issues are often initially disagreed upon in negotiations because their value is subjective. For example, company A may value their time at a much higher clip than company B thinks it is worth.

Conditions: Circumstances that must be met in order for a contract or deal to be completed.

Contractor: A person hired to do work for someone else but who is not an employee or agent of that person.

Courage: One of the five psychological pressure points in negotiating. Courage is the mental or moral strength to venture, persevere, or withstand danger, fear, intimidation, or difficulty so as to strike the best deal possible for your business. Mental strength is a direct result of knowledge, practice and success. Gradually, a small amount of courage will grow and your success in negotiations will increase.

D

Deficiency: Something lacking; a skill or resource that requires improvement.

Desire: A longing for something. In business, a motivational force and occasional liability for an overeager negotiator.

Disagreement: A common obstacle in negotiations where one party is unsatisfied with a proposed arrangement.

Disarming: A ploy by which one side, if put on the defensive, deflects and quells the aggressor's actions.

Discipline: The patience and resolve to better one's self through rigorous study and work habits. Good discipline is closely linked to having a solid mind-set and requires courage and a firm understanding of one's business. Good discipline keeps a negotiator on track and making fair deals, rather than settling for less than what he or she needs.

Discussion: In negotiating, a conversation where the aim is to arrive at a mutual understanding and agreement.

Dispute: See *Disagreement*.

E

Enforceable agreement: A contract; an agreement that is enforceable by law, where one party may take action against the other if the agreement is not satisfied.

Estimate: A tool used in business to gauge the preliminary or approximate value of a good or service.

Ethics: A factor in determining your bargaining issues, ethics has to do with right and wrong in business practice. Ethical values should not be compromised.

Evaluation: One of the four stages of negotiation where a negotiator reviews relevant facts to determine how they may influence his or her negotiation.

Expenses: Costs or charges a business must cover in order to operate.

F

Fair deal: A fair deal occurs when both sides of a negotiation are satisfied, even if the end result is not exactly what either had initially hoped for. As long as neither side is grossly taken advantage of and both sides benefit, a deal is considered to be fair.

Fear: One of the five psychological pressure points in negotiating. The fear factor comes into play when your judgment is focused on not losing rather than getting your fair due. This is what makes novice negotiators accept poor terms and keeps them from reaching fair deals. Fear must be overcome for a negotiator to be successful.

Financial resources: Money and other liquefiable assets that are available for a person or business to spend. Having more financial resources allows for more flexibility in negotiations.

Financial status: A person or business's financial strength or wellbeing. Having access to this information can provide leverage in negotiations.

Flinching: Often combined with the **Bold Response** tactic, a flinch is a visual cue intended to convey a message or emotion to another person.

Fortuitous power: A chance circumstance that lends a temporary advantage to one side. This usually involves timing or having an edge as a supplier.

"Funny money": A payment offer made by a potential buyer that is laughably low. In some cases this low offer is because the buyer is ignorant of your service's true value, or because the buyer is testing to see how low you are willing to settle. In either case, the offer must be tactfully declined. When receiving a laughable offer, break the payment down to understandable units of time and costs to show the prospect how the money doesn't warrant the time and effort involved.

G

Good cop: The foil of the bad cop, the good cop in a negotiation tries to befriend the other party to gain a psychological advantage and win their cooperation.

Good cop bad cop: A tactic used by two buyers where one is difficult (the bad cop) and the other seems amiable, apologetic, and interested in getting a deal done (the good cop). The ploy is designed to make the other party more lenient on their own position in order to repay the good cop's kindness.

Gross negligence: The conscious and voluntary disregard of reasonable care, which is likely to cause foreseeable injury or harm to persons or property.

Groundwork: Preliminary preparations that must be made before taking on a new job or enterprise.

H

Hard negotiator: Like an aggressive buyer, someone who is very direct in negotiations, makes no attempt to befriend the other party, makes difficult demands, displays a resistance to compromise, speaks loudly, uses intimidation tactics, and seems as unapproachable as a mother tiger guarding her cubs.

"Hidden costs": The costs of doing business beyond what one anticipates. These include hours invested to make a sale, grief from the buyer, and maybe even having the word get out that special deals can be cut.

Hold-harmless clause: Part of a legal contract stating that an individual or organization is not liable for any injuries or damages caused to the individual signing the contract.

Homework sheet: A form that lists the important details of a negotiation and stimulates thinking.

Hostility: The product of a serious conflict, which often requires resolution through negotiation. Differences of opinion do not usually cause hostility unless they are rooted in some ideology that prevents the parties from accommodating one another's point of view.

I

Ideology: A fundamental and often irreconcilable life view that can create roadblocks in negotiations.

Indemnification clause: A sentence in a contract stating that the signer with be compensated for any damage or losses sustained.

Inherent power: Power that is bestowed by circumstance, the most common types being financial power and official power.

Intermediary: A go-between third party who aids negotiations between two other parties.

Intimidation: An aggressive negotiation tactic that can be effective if the aggressor has leverage; however, it can also backfire.

Investigation: The first of the four stages of negotiation in which information about a prospective client is gathered in order to create an effective approach and realistic goals for when the negotiations begin.

M

Margin: A monetary amount allowed or available beyond what is actually necessary. A savvy negotiator will get as much as possible.

"Meeting of the minds": A latter stage in the negotiation process where each party tries to understand and meet the other's position. A meeting of the minds results in a mutual understanding only when the parties are reasonable and willing to be flexible.

Morals: See *Ethics*.

Motivation: One of the five psychological pressure points in negotiating. Motivation is the reason for every business decision.

N

Necessity: Something that is required for a business to function.

Negotiating: The process of moving back and forth between wants and needs until each party agrees that an acceptable balance between all the parties' wants and needs has been achieved.

Negotiation planning: The preliminary steps taken and research conducted before beginning a negotiation.

Nibbling: A tactic that can be employed after a deal has been struck in which one party teases out additional value for itself.

Non-negotiable: A point that cannot be changed and must be agreed upon in order for a deal to go forward. No matter how firm they may seem, these positions should always be challenged.

O

Optional offer: A secondary offer made by a negotiator when the client is unable to accept the first proposal. An optional offer effectively solves the problem the client had with the first offer so that a deal can be reached.

Oral contract: A verbal (as opposed to written) agreement.

Out-of-pocket payments: Payments that are fronted by an individual using his or her own financial resources. For obvious reasons, out-of-pocket payments are best avoided whenever possible.

Overhead: One of the four value issues for negotiating services, overhead is the fixed cost of running a business.

P

Parameters: Guidelines to follow in a negotiation.

Payment: The exchange of money for a good or service.

Position: An idea of dollar value for concrete issues like a good or service, which may differ from the other party's view. Understanding and trying to accommodate one another's positions is a key to facilitating negotiations.

Position bargaining: A type of bargaining involving concrete issues such as money, materials, and time.

Positive priming: A tactic by which one conditions someone else to say yes.

Power: The ability to act or produce an effect. One of the five psychological pressure points in negotiating.

"Pressure points": The five psychological pressure points in negotiating: power, fear, risk, courage, and mind-set. These must all be managed for effective negotiating.

Principle bargaining: Involves abstract issues, such as your business policies.

Priorities: A ranking of a person's wants and needs from most to least important.

Profit: Financial gain and excess after bottom-line requirements have been met.

Prospect: A prospective client or business partner.

R

Reality check: During a negotiation, the act of stepping back from one's work to make sure that one's goals and expectations are practical.

Rebuttal: A response or counteroffer.

Red herring: A non-issue meant to distract the other party form the real issues. See also *Straw man*.

Refusal: A tactic used to halt negotiations from advancing.

Relationship: Refers to how well two entities do business with each other and how willing they are to continue their partnership.

Risk: The chance involved in a deal and the potential loss or benefits that go with it.

S

Soft negotiator: A negotiator who is very friendly, tries to befriend the other party, and makes no demands but rather offers suggestions, pushes compromise to make the deal, has a friendly tone of voice, appears to be tranquil, and tries to make his or her opponent think he or she is working in the opponent's best interest.

"Straw man": A sham argument meant to be defeated. It is like a red herring in negotiating; that is, not a real issue but something brought in to influence outcomes.

Style: A person's approach to a negotiation and his or her adaptability when working with different kinds of clients.

T

Tactical goals: The objectives one is trying to achieve by using a specific tactic.

Tactical negotiating: Employing any number of techniques to improve one's position in a negotiation. Whenever negotiations reach roadblocks, tactics are necessary to get things moving again.

Terms and conditions: Details that both sides must agree upon before a contract can be finalized. May include deadlines, deposits, expense reimbursements, and insurance requirements.

Time-shift: A solution to scheduling conflicts. For example, when a client requests work on a date for which the provider of the service is booked. Rather than postpone the already scheduled job, the provider may ask the new client to let him or her provide the service on a different day. This allows the provider to make money he or she would not otherwise receive and show the client that his or her time is in demand and therefore valuable.

Trade-off: In negotiating, an arrangement by which one gives up one advantageous position for another.

Trading: In negotiations, an exchange of goods and services that are usually considered to be of approximately equal value.

Trial balloon: A tactic used to test the waters without putting one's client on the spot. For example, presenting a hypothetical scenario.

U

Understanding: Agreement between two parties.

V

Value level: How one party sees the dollar value of the goods or services being provided. See also *Position*.

W

"Whew" price: The selling price of a good or service that satisfies one's bottom line. The "whew" price is what you need to stay in business.

"Whoopee" price: The selling price of a good or service that exceeds what one needs to stay in business. Ideally, this is the price you want to sell for.

Willful negligence: Performance of a careless act in disregard of a known risk; conscious indifference to consequences.

"Win-win": A situation where a negotiation ends with each party receiving what they agree is fair value for fair value.

Wrapping up: The end of a negotiation, at which point a contract is usually signed.

Written contract: A document that summarizes and details all the terms and conditions agreed upon by both parties during verbal negotiations. These contracts are signed by both parties and become legally binding so that each party must fulfill their end of the agreement.

INDEX

Books from Allworth Press

Allworth Press is an imprint of Skyhorse Publishing, Inc. Selected titles are listed below.

Pocket Small Business Owner's Guide to Building Your Business
by Kevin Devine (5½ x 8¼, 256 pages, paperback, $14.95)

The Entrepreneurial Age
by Larry C. Farrell (6.69 x 9.61, 252 pages, paperback, $27.50)

The Pocket Legal Companion to Trademark: A User-Friendly Handbook on Avoiding Lawsuits and Protecting Your Trademarks
by Lee Wilson (5 x 7½, 320 pages, paperback, $16.95)

The Pocket Legal Companion to Copyright: A User-Friendly Handbook for Profiting from Copyrights
by Lee Wilson (5 x 7½, 320 pages, paperback, $16.95)

Emotional Branding, Revised Edition: The New Paradigm for Connecting Brands to People
by Marc Grobe (6 x 9, 344 pages, paperback, $24.95)

The Art of Digital Branding, Revised Edition
by Ian Cocoran (6 x 9, 272 pages, paperback, $23.95)

Turn Your Idea or Invention into Millions
by Don Kracke (6 x 9, 224 pages, paperback, $18.95)

Legal Forms for Everyone, Fifth Edition
by Carl W. Battle (8½ x 11, 240 pages, paperback, $24.95)

Your Living Trust and Estate Plan, 2012-2013: How to Maximize Your Family's Assets and Protect Your Loved Ones
by Harvey J. Platt (6 x 9, 352 pages, paperback, $23.95)

Power Speaking: The Art of the Exceptional Public Speaker
by Achim Nowak (6 x 9, 256 pages, paperback, $19.95)

To see our complete catalog or to order online, please visit *www.allworth.com*.